Emilia Plater
&
the November Uprising

Emilia Plater
&
the November Uprising
A Heroic Young Countess and the Struggle
of Polish Independence, 1830–31

Josef Straszewicz

With a Short Illustrated Account of the
Battle of Warsaw 6–7 September 1831
by A. S. Krause

LEONAUR

Emilia Plater & the November Uprising
A Heroic Young Countess and the Struggle of Polish Independence, 1830-31
by Josef Straszewicz
With a Short Illustrated Account of the Battle of Warsaw 6-7 September 1831
by A. S. Krause

FIRST EDITION

First published under the title
Life of the Countess Emilia Plater

Leonaur is an imprint of Oakpast Ltd

Copyright in this form © 2017 Oakpast Ltd

ISBN: 978-1-78282-640-8 (hardcover)
ISBN: 978-1-78282-641-5 (softcover)

http://www.leonaur.com

Publisher's Notes

Contents

EMILY PLATER

Author's Preface

Among the many instances of devotedness and patriotism which the late Polish revolution has afforded us, that of Emily Plater occupies the first rank. Her name excites a thrill of emotion in every heart which is not insensible to feelings of honour and patriotism. Everyone has heard of Emily Plater's serving as a soldier in the national cause, and of her dying, while yet in the prime of life, in the service of her country.

But the particulars of a life so beautiful and so romantic have as yet been wanting to us. Connected with the Countess Plater by old family ties, proprietor of an estate in the neighbourhood of her own, and her companion in arms on the plains of Lithuania, I have followed the heroine through her whole career, have been made the confident of her thoughts, and have shared in her dangers. Her whole life is well known to me. I have seen Emily, in her earliest youth, fondly muse upon the glory of Poland as others would upon a lover; and cherish the remembrances connected with our ancient nationality until they became almost the objects of her idolatry. I have seen the young girl grow up, and with her these noble recollections. It was no difficult thing to foresee that, when the clarion of battle should sound, Emily would join the ranks as a soldier, and wield the lance.

Her military companions were mine, and I have been present at the same dangers. Later, when proscribed and cast on the Prussian soil, I was compelled to seek an asylum in France, I lost sight of her. Then, overcome by her long-continued fatigues, she was approaching her end. At the early age of twenty-six she paid the forfeit to which the dreams of her ardent and almost supernatural enthusiasm had exposed her. But the particulars of her death have reached me. I have received letters dated from her sick chamber, and I have personally questioned those who closed her eyes.

I am thus in possession of all the materials requisite for the biographical sketch of the heroine, which I propose as an offering to her admirers, in order that she may be the more beloved as she becomes more extensively known. Besides, it is quite time that a correct version should supersede and rectify the multitude of fabulous accounts, which, until this time, have fed European credulity.

My first intention was to insert these remarks in my work entitled, *The Polish men and women of the revolution of 29th November, 1830, &c.*, but, already overwhelmed with materials, I deemed it best to publish this biography separately.

The article under the title of *The Countess Plater*, in my biographical work, will be a summary of the present biography which I am now about to offer to the public; for this volume will contain all, even the most minute details, of her short, but glorious life.

May my ability prove adequate to the task which I have assumed, as a faithful narrator of all that is noble and generous in the valiant heart of woman.

CHAPTER 1

Birth of Emily

A celebrated writer says:

Circumstances do not make men, but serve to develop them.

With man is born the seed of his future being—of his virtues and of his vices, of his greatness and of his crimes. If propensities to evil are born with him, his life will develop and bring into activity that germ of evil which lay dormant in the recesses of his heart. If, on the other hand, dispositions to the good and to the sublime in action are innate with him, his life will be great and good. Still his future will always owe much to events, and these alone will prove what he is, or, at least, what he appears to be. Every political crisis, every political commotion, has been the means of producing some of these vigorous minds, who, thirsting for fame, wait only for the signal, an opportunity to rush forward, seize the command and direction of popular movements, and become the head and soul, the tyrant or the protector, the destroyer or the benefactor.

Such men are not the real causes of the events which bring them forward into notice. These events are sometimes the effects of pure chance, but much oftener of necessity. They are inevitable, because consequent on the progress of the society in which they shine forth. It is at such times the passions ferment,—ambition, the desire of advancement, occupies the soul, and he who is inspired with lofty sentiments, and with ideas at once noble and useful, and which respond to the wants of the epoch, is soon borne onward to his proper place, the head of the multitude.

How pleasing to follow, step by step, the career of such beings; to trace their noble and devoted lives, and to propose them as models for the rising generations of oppressed nations!

Generally obscure in their origin, and coming forth from the bosom of the people—a suffering people, and one which is awakened to the anticipation of a happier future, the progress of such men is gradual. They elevate themselves by degrees above the multitude with which, for a time, they are confounded, and of which they finally become the leaders. They are thought embodied, the exponent of the movement; they defend a nation's rights, vindicate and secure its future peace. Apostles of liberty, they preach by speech or by the sword, and nations gather around them, listen to them with respect, and follow them as priests and kings.

Sometimes, too, they fall in their dangerous career. Betrayed by circumstances, they leave in a state of incompleteness, or of entire ruin, the work which they have undertaken. They moisten with their blood the land which they would deliver, and while cursed by the conqueror, who brands them with the names of robber and rebel, they are invoked as martyrs by the oppressed. Martyrs in the cause of liberty, they merit, too, palms and crowns; for it should not be imputed to them as a fault that victory has not crowned their efforts—fortune, not courage, has failed them.

The remembrance of these glorious men, and the recital of their exploits, are long the consolation of the vanquished. Under the tent, and around the fireside, their history is again and again recounted, and their heroic actions, deeply cherished, will, at some future day, give birth to new heroes, who will follow in their footsteps, and under the guidance of a more propitious fortune, will perhaps accomplish the great work in whose cause their predecessors sacrificed their lives.

What nation has suffered more than the Poles, in the effort to maintain their rights and independence? What nation, within the space of half a century, has made fiercer struggles or shed more blood upon their native soil? There is not a city, nor a hamlet in the land, which has not witnessed great deeds, and there is not a furrow which has not been fertilized by the blood of illustrious victims.

It is for history to record the names of these champions of the freedom of a great people—religiously to preserve the memory of their deeds, and to transmit them to an inquisitive and admiring posterity, of all that is great and generous inhuman action.

We propose to trace the life of one of the thousand heroes that Poland has produced, in her struggles against slavery and cruelty. It is the life of a woman that we propose to recount, but of a woman who, in courage and patriotism, has never been surpassed, even by man. This

10

woman is Emily Plater—a heroine, if ever a woman existed worthy of the name. Who has not heard of this glorious name? What heart has not glowed with admiration at the recital of the exploits of this young Polish female?

The family of Emily Plater, one of the most extensive and well known in Poland, derives its origin from Westphalia, in Germany. At the commencement of the thirteenth century, when the Christian world was engaged in spreading far and wide the religion of Jesus Christ, one of the family of the Platers passed over into Livonia, as knight of the order of *sword-bearers*, in order to convert to Christianity, the idolatrous inhabitants. From that time the name of Plater frequently occurs in the annals of that country, and they have enjoyed that influence in it which the twofold advantage of immense wealth, and a nobility whose origin mounts up to a remote antiquity, can confer. The order of sword-bearers,—sometimes the ally, at others the enemy of Poland,—at last claimed the protection of this country against the cruel Ivan Vassilievitsch, *Tzar* of Moscow, who was ravaging Livonia.

In 1561, Gothard Kettler, the grand master of the order, did homage and swore allegiance to Sigismond Augustus, king of Poland, and Livonia became a Polish province. In succeeding times the Platers proved, by their patriotism, that they were worthy of bearing the name of Poles. One of the family, Sigismond, covered his name with glory by a heroic death, in defence of the city of Dünabourg, against the Muscovites. As a reward for his bravery the Republic gave to his family the Staroste of Dünabourg, which remained in the possession of the Counts Plater until 1820, when they were arbitrarily deprived of it by the Russian government. (To be named Staroste, was to receive for life, or in perpetuity, a fief of the crown).

And finally, in our last struggle against despotism, many members of this family distinguished themselves by their devotedness to the Polish cause, sacrificing everything to the freedom and happiness of their country. If they were not successful, they at least have nothing to reproach themselves with.

But the person who has shed upon this family the brightest ray of glory, is, without question, Emily Plater, whose history we are now about to commence.

She was born at Wilna, on the 13th Nov. 1806. Her father, Count Xavier Plater, married in 18—, the Countess Anna de Mohl, a young heiress, possessing, in an eminent degree, all that can render a woman distinguished in society or in the domestic circle. Gentle, well educated, virtuous and affectionate, she sought nothing but the happiness and the affection of those who surrounded her.

Unfortunately, she did not meet, in her husband, with that peace and felicity to which she was so justly entitled. She was obliged to separate from him, and retire, in 1815, into Livonia, to the residence of a distant relative, taking with her her daughter, who from that epoch became her sole source of consolation, and to the education of whom she devoted her whole time.

CHAPTER 2

Her Character

Madame Lieberg (for this was the name of the relative to whom Emily's mother retired) was the widow of a late chamberlain of Livonia. She was already advanced in age, without children, and in possession of a very ample fortune, which she employed chiefly in doing good. The poor never left her door without succour, and never did a friend in need seek her aid in vain. Respected by her family, of whom she was almost the head, the oracle of her neighbours, who cherished in her the benefactress of the district, a mother to her tenantry, whose children she educated, she enjoyed universal esteem.

The mother of Emily was received by her kinswoman with that lively interest with which the sight of unmerited misfortune always inspires a benevolent heart. Possessing in a high degree all that is pleasing in a child—simplicity, candour, a sweet and affable temper and an ingenuous mind—the young Emily soon gained the heart of her old relative, who loved her as her own child. The domain of Madame Lieberg is situated in the Polish Livonia, which, since the invasion of Poland by the Tzarina Catharine, has constituted a part of the government of Witebsk.

The residence of a wealthy individual, Lixna, with all its rural edifices and dependencies, presents the appearance of a great castle. It is situated upon a hill, near the bank of a small stream flowing into the Dzwina, whose majestic course may be descried at a great distance. The situation itself is one of the most beautiful that can be imagined. In the immediate vicinity, everything is gay, lively and smiling, and the eye is deeply gratified. But on the right, there extends a vast forest of black fir, whose sombre shade, brought into immediate contrast with the scene just described, serves as a sort of finish to the beauty of the landscape.

The interior of this stately mansion, the residence of its proprietor, involuntarily transports us to former times. Everything in it bears the impress of a simple and severe, but foreign and antique taste. There you will find, still existing, the eighteenth century with its pretensions, its odd decorations, and 'its artificial character.

The principal edifice is built in a style which defies description. It is not surrounded with deep trenches, neither is the access to it through a heavy and unwieldy drawbridge; but it is, even to this day, enclosed by a long and massive wall; and turrets, inoffensive indeed, occupy each of its corners. It is no longer a feudal castle, and it is as far from being a modern palace. It is the architecture of our own times intermingled with that of the middle ages—the eighteenth century wedded to the fifteenth.

It is surrounded by a vast garden, or rather immense park, where gracefulness and the pleasing simplicity of nature are sought for in vain. In it almost everything is spoiled by art; it is, in fine, the old French garden, with its symmetrical espaliers, its walks and plots geometrically laid out, and trees fantastically trimmed in conformity with every possible shape but that of nature. At one of the extremities is a labyrinth—rather a frigid imitation of an English park—whose paths are carefully laid out, which, crossing each other, diverging and shooting in a thousand different ways in the most perplexing manner, serve to lead astray whoever may venture into them.

In one word, gardens, buildings, and all that belongs to this domain, even to the servants grown old in the service of their masters, bear in their antiquity a venerable though mournful aspect. The lady of the manor, who has taken care to preserve ancient customs, has not forgotten the frank and cordial hospitality of the old Polish nobility, and that politeness of theirs which was less prodigal of words than of deeds.

In this abode, Emily Plater passed the greater part of her brief existence. Here she received from her kinswoman and mother examples of private virtues the most exalted.

The quiet and monotonous life of the castle increased her natural propensity to melancholy; and the antique aspect of all that surrounded her, stamped her character with that masculine energy which she displayed at the time of the insurrection. It was here likewise that she received her education.

Emily, from her earliest years, evinced tastes of a very different character from those generally displayed by young persons of her age and sex. The doll and the other playthings of children never afforded her any pleasure, and the dance for her had no attractions; she could not conceive, even, how it could be a source of pleasure to others. The soft and effeminate music of the saloon made but slight impression upon a soul which required emotions of greater strength and passion. Drawing was more to her taste; but it was in nature that she sought her models, and not in pictures themselves, the copies of other copies. It was in solitude, under the open sky and in the depths of the forest, that she sought her inspirations.

Her education then was quite unlike that generally received by persons of her sex. She required that which would nourish the affections of the heart—things of a serious character, and not senseless trifles. As soon as she arrived at an age in which she was at liberty to direct her own studies, she entirely threw aside everything which belongs to a young girl, and sought occupations more befitting her character.

The study, which possessed the greatest attractions for her, was history. She loved to see the ages, which are passed, move in long array, with their attendant virtues and crimes, before her. She seemed to herself actually to take part in the great drama of the human race, so abundant in intrigues and schemes for self-aggrandizement. She pursued the progressive march of opinions, and studied men as well as nations. Her heart kindled with admiration for all that was great and noble.

And to these qualities, what nation in the world could, for her, possess stronger claims than Poland, her country, the free, the faithful, the generous Poland; that Poland so proud of its freedom, and which was already civilized when the rest of Europe was scarcely removed from a state of barbarism; which was free when all other nations were enslaved; the firm barrier against the encroachments of Islamism, and which was always brave, and prepared to succour the oppressed, even without hope of reward; a country which fell, at last, a victim to the ingratitude of its neighbour's, of which the one owed to her its existence, and the other its preservation; a country, in fine, which, even in its fall, has forced from the rest of the world the mingled feelings of admiration and regret.

Emily Plater read the annals of this heroic nation, whose pages are replete with those precepts of devotedness and examples of sacrifices, which the country expects from her children in times of danger. These, with the bloody record of the massacres of Praga, produced in her heart a just hatred against her country's oppressors, whose iniquitous government was by no means calculated to conciliate the good will of a people conquered and kept in submission by force of arms.

In Poland, female education is deemed of more serious importance than in other countries. Females learn that they are children of Poland before they learn that they are women. Their education is eminently patriotic, and perhaps more national than that bestowed upon the men. Their understandings are formed with a view to future usefulness to their country.

If we trace back our history to its source, we shall find a Wanda sacrificing her life for the country. Although perhaps a fabulous personage, yet she has been to our Polish heroines the model of their adoption, and they scrupulously follow her example.

We learn, from our old traditions, that no woman could aspire to matrimony until she had imbrued her hand in the blood of her nation's foreign oppressors. Evidence of this is transmitted to us by our writers. The learned author of *Women, their condition and their social influence among different nations both ancient and modern*, says:

> The Sarmatian women ride on horseback, and accompany their husbands in the chase and in their expeditions; on which occasions they wear the same dress. As to matrimony, no one can aspire to it before she can prove that she has killed an enemy with her own hand. It often happens that they attain to an advanced age before they are married.

The love of country, and the hatred of foreign domination, have always been the predominant qualities of the ancient Sarmatian women.

The young and beautiful Hedwige (1384—1399), who was wholly devoted to the happiness of Poland, impatient of the Hungarian yoke, and exasperated by the depredations they were committing in the Russian territories, placed herself at the head of an army and drove them away. She regained possession, by storm or capitulation, of Przemysl, Jaroslaw, Grodck, Halicz, Trembowla and Leopol; and while with one hand she wielded the sword, with the other she protected the arts and sciences, and to her is the University of Cracow indebted for its greatness and its celebrity.

Among the females who have swayed the sceptre of Poland, the names of Hedwige, of Elizabeth, and of Helena, will forever live in the memory of man.

When the immortal Stephen Czarniecki, the saviour of Poland, under John Casimir (1556), left his peaceful home to go against the Swedes, his daughter, Alexandra Catharina Czarniecka, bitterly wept that her tender age would not allow her to fight by the side of her father, whose glory and danger she was so very anxious to share.

The mother of Henry II. duke of Breslaw, in putting into the hands of her son the Polish sabre, which he was to use against the Tartars, spoke these memorable words:

My son, if you wish that I should not disown you, run to the defence of our dear country.

The virtuous Sobieska, greeting her sons on their return from foreign countries, pronounced these words:

It is with unspeakable joy I see you again, but I would disown you as my children, were you to imitate the base cowardice of those who deserted the field of battle near Pilawce.

And with what admiration have we not contemplated the resolute Chrianowska, whose courage saved Trembowla (1674), which her unworthy husband wished to surrender to the Turks, by whom it was besieged!

The princess Radziwill (1764) was always found by the side of her brother, the prince Charles, in the midst of the most bloody contests, and fought as bravely as the bravest soldier; and she finally selected for her husband, him who had been the most distinguished in battle.

When, in the year 1792, the infamous treason of Targowica had rendered nugatory all that had been done by the Polish patriots, his chief, Stanislas Felix Potocki, who had sold himself to the Muscovites, had the audacity to write a congratulatory letter to his aunt, the Countess of Kamieniec, on the advent of a new year, the sublime answer she made him is such as no Polish woman will ever forget.

Oh thou, whoever thou art (for I deny thy right to the title thou hast assumed), thou who hast had the audacity to raise thy impious arm against thy country—thou, who through an unworthy ambition of showing what thou wast capable of, hast not blushed to seek, through means so iniquitous and shameful, the oppression of thy fellow citizens, tremble! . . . . . thou art the sole author of thy own misery, thou hast brought upon thyself thy own ruin—the ignominy and shame which will overwhelm thee—thou hast wrought thy own destruction.
Those shots which thou hast caused to be cast in thy own fur-

nace, shall be turned against thee. That steel, which thy parri-cidal hand hast sharpened against thy country, shall be plunged to the hilt into thy own bosom. Thou hast sought thy own sordid interest, and that of thy infamous accomplice, by betray-ing an innocent people to oppression. But listen to what Divine Wisdom has in store for thee. I shall confound thy counsels, I shall defeat thy sacrilegious projects; I shall cause all thy plans to miscarry; thou shalt be an object of derision and of popular indignation—thou shalt lead a life of wo, forsaken by the for-eigner, and exposed to the dreadful and inevitable vengeance of thy own country.

And the accomplishment of this dreadful denunciation is now matter of history. (We have extracted this letter from the precious col-lection of fragments of the cotemporary history of Poland by Leonard Chodzko).

The Duchess of Würtemberg, Princess Czartoryska by birth, sepa-rated herself from her husband, 1792, because he served in the army of the enemies of Poland, and some time afterwards disowned her own son for the same cause.

What devotedness did not those admirable women display in the war for national independence in 1794, under Kosciuszko! When the news of the Hero of Poland having been made prisoner on the field of battle, at Maciëiowice, reached Warsaw, it caused more than forty miscarriages; the acuteness of this national calamity was more than so frail an organisation could sustain.

It would be wandering from the intended limits of our subject were we to speak here of the patriotism of the Polish women in 1806, 9, 12 and 13, as well as that previous to the late revolution and dur-ing its continuance. The records of such facts may be found in almost every page of Poland's history, which will transmit to posterity the names of those remarkable women, as it will also that of Emily Plater, and many other heroines, who distinguished themselves in the late struggle of Poland against her oppressors. Who has not heard of the patriotic benevolence of Emily Szczaniecka, of Cunegonde Ogin-ska, of Claudine Potocka, and so many other Polish, Lithuanian and Russian women? In Poland, courage is the delight of women, and devotedness to the state is as common among them as it is rare among other nations.

Towards the end of 1820, a great commotion took place among

the enslaved nations. Many made an attempt to regain those rights of which they had been deprived, and vindicate that liberty whose inestimable price then began to be felt. A shout of independence was heard from the shores of the Eurotes to the banks of the Orinoco—on the Olympus and on the Cordilleras. Sublime and electric shock! which roused from their lethargy, nations who had been so long languishing in slavery! In many countries, this burst of enthusiasm for independence, was suppressed, and whole nations relapsed into those fetters they had endeavoured to break.

On the other hand, some were more fortunate, and with more perseverance and courage, because their sufferings were perhaps more intolerant, left the field as conquerors, and after great sacrifices, as the price of their long struggles, restored freedom to their country. At the head of these is the ancient nation of the Hellenes, who shook off the heavy yoke of the Turks and regained their nationality.—Emily Plater, whose greatest delight was to hear the shout of freedom, ardently espoused the Greek cause. She shared the general enthusiasm of Europe in favour of this heroic nation. She anxiously followed the progress of their insurrection, and envied the destiny of the heroine of Missolonghi.

She said:

Men, in the course of their duty, can but challenge death. Bobelina goes beyond—she braves public opinion besides.

But it was Joan of Arc who was the principal idol of her enthusiasm. Joan of Arc, that inspired virgin, that extraordinary woman who rescued France from the grasp of its enemies, whose invasion had been permitted by its indolent and feeble monarch. She made the life of this woman her favourite study. She sought all the works of those days which had any reference to this event, and read them often. She found a great analogy between France under English oppression, and Poland groaning under the Russian yoke.

Her closet was filled with engravings representing that heroine in the different phases of her life; she became the object of her veneration as well as the subject of her dreams. Envious of her fame, her most ardent wish was to rival her, and do for Poland, at some future day, that which Joan had formerly accomplished for France. This was her whole ambition. She often spoke of it; and men, in their wisdom, turned into ridicule what they were pleased to term her foolish extravagance; because they could not understand, nor would they ever

19

have understood her, had not the events of 1830 kindled the fire of patriotism in every Polish bosom.

Emily was not satisfied with the expression of vain wishes only, but she took the necessary measures to put them in execution at some future time. Her favourite amusements and ordinary exercises now consisted in riding on horseback, shooting at a mark, and inuring herself to the rigors of the seasons and to every temperature. The countess, fearing for the health of her daughter, attempted at first to put a stop to this kind of exercise; but Emily, by her fond caresses, overcame her mother's fears, and finally obtained from her that consent she had so earnestly solicited. From that time, this young amazon would be seen to spring into the saddle, leap over ditches, dart through the fields, and even penetrate the forest. She seemed to be indefatigable, and nothing could stop her.

In the saloon, she was apparently sad, pensive, and even melancholy; the etiquette and cold formalities of society were irksome to her, and seemed to send a chill into her ardent soul. But mounted on her favourite courser, she would boldly wander over the fields—practise at shooting, brave the severity of the elements, snow, or rain, or the burning heat of the sun; and when in her rides, it became necessary to face danger, then would she display the whole energy of her character.

It was thus that she inured and prepared herself for the great day of battles,—that day, when, in answer to the shout of Warsaw for independence, all would rush to arms—that day she so ardently desired, and which she apparently foresaw, although nothing had as yet taken place even to excite a suspicion that such an event was so near at hand.

CHAPTER 3

Condemnation

In the meantime, the persecution of the Russian Government reached a member of the family of our heroine. Her first cousin, Michael Plater, was condemned to serve in the Russian Army in the quality of a private soldier. In order to explain the motives of this outrageous sentence, it is necessary to say a few words on the subject of the hostility of the pretended conqueror of Napoleon against the Lithuanian youth, and which he carried on in so secret a manner as to escape the observation of the historians of the reign of the Emperor Alexander, although it has caused the misery and ruin of a whole nation.

Alexander, the pupil of Laharp, was both a despot and a philanthropist; of an irresolute character, he, for a considerable time, wavered between the principles of his tutor and that policy which has constantly governed the princes of his dynasty.

One hand he extended to the protection of literature, while he employed the other ill crushing civilization. Besides, he reigned at a time when the crowned heads of Europe, under pretence of liberal principles, were doing all in their power to arrest the progress of liberty, as well as the career of Napoleon, whose ostensible cause for carrying on war against them was the affranchisement of nations. It was then the King of Prussia promised his subjects a constitutional government; and even Metternich himself ceased to get in a passion at the mere mention or name of liberty, and even went so far as to extend his protection to secret associations.

In 1815, the kings, who no longer had anything to fear from their great foe, cast off their masks and formed, what they were pleased to call, their Holy Alliance against the Jacobins and demagogues whom they had so well succeeded in cajoling. It was then that Alexander, the chief of this league, came to a final decision; the lust of despotism prevailed over his philanthropy; he even regretted the little good he had done before, and from this moment began the demolition of his own work.

The events of 1812 clearly proved that the Polish provinces of his empire, conquered but not subdued, could not be retained in subjection, except by main force, and that the desire of regaining their former independence pervaded every heart. In order to eradicate this nationality, which was incompatible with his own views, he trampled underfoot all his solemn engagements—violated the laws of the country—proscribed the Polish language, and established in all the tribunals the Russian practice—an object of general detestation. A few learned publicists and profound historians have already passed their judgments upon this glaring violation of a charter solemnly granted, and of institutions whose maintenance had been sworn to before the whole world. The author of such deeds has covered himself with infamy; the tyrant and the perfidious can never escape general contempt and hatred. Such a triumph as his, is worse than a glorious defeat.

Nevertheless, the mighty will of this despot has been baffled by the firmness of the national spirit; his ukases were powerless, and generally evaded. Prince Czartoryski, chief of public instruction in these provinces, did all in his power to circumvent and defeat all his obnoxious designs, and to preserve the Polish nationality. Even his enemy, Nowosiltzoff, has been known to say that one year of the prince's administration was sufficient to neutralise the efforts of ten years on the part of the Autocrat and his spies against liberty.

The University of Wilna was a nursery which the Polish youth never quitted without being wholly devoted to their country, heart and soul. Lelewell was professor of history there; his extensive knowledge, and profound researches enabled him to fill that chair with superior credit. His fame and eloquence drew a crowd of auditors to his lectures, to which he knew how to impart that liberal and patriotic spirit which pervades all his writings, and which influenced all the actions of his life. He always ended by making these young men, ardently desirous of knowledge and fame, warm patriots, and devoted friends of knowledge and independence. Thomas Zan, Adam Mickiewicz, Leonard Chodzko, Michael Wollowicz, and some other distinguished Polish youth were among his pupils.

Although the spirit of opposition pervaded the whole nation, yet concert of action was needed, and in order to oppose the scheme of government with some hope of success, it became necessary to organise a corps, or association, whose members could obtain the confidence and direction of public opinion. Thomas Zan caught hold of this idea, and immediately put it in execution by organising a club called the *Radiants*, whose objects were to propagate knowledge, maintain the use of their vernacular tongue, at any risk, and defend their nationality against violence. This association, which was joined by most of the students of the university, gave umbrage to the government, who began their persecution in 1821 by the issue of an ukase for its dissolution.

Zan and his associates, far from being discouraged by these proceedings, reunited a second time under the name of *Philarethiians*, and a second time they were dispersed. They again rallied, but in a smaller number, and under the name of *Philomatians*. The animosity displayed by the Russian Government in this instance, sufficiently proved the utility of their society in teaching them perseverance; and consequently, they reorganised their society upon a much larger plan, but kept their meetings more secret. To cultivate literature and the sciences, to dissipate opinions prejudicial to the welfare of their country, to imbue every heart with patriotism and love of freedom—such were the noble objects this association proposed to itself. This association, composed, as it was, of the greatest part of the most intelligent young men in Poland, under the direction of Thomas Zan, a man of the most energetic character and daring mind, was perfectly adequate to the performance of the duties its members had imposed upon themselves.

Lithuania already began to feel the benefit of these noble operations; a typographical association was formed for the cheap publication of Polish works; these were followed by the organisation of a society which had for its object the affording to indigent, but industrious young men, the means of pursuing their studies; a third one undertook to prepare a correct and minute digest of the statistics of the Polish provinces, whose inhabitants, till that time plunged in apathy, were soon lost in amazement at the immense advantage they derived from these labours—a result which any single individual would have sought to effect in vain. This association succeeded, through their unremitting efforts, in remodelling the national character, and dissipating existing prejudices—the value of labour began to be appreciated, and industry was no longer deemed degrading.

Such was their mode of conducting their secret operations against despotism. Zan was well aware of the physical impossibility of success

Thomas Zan

in a premature struggle with the giant of the north, and that such a movement, far from being of any service to the country, would only ensure the subversion of all his plans. He therefore limited his efforts to strengthening his countrymen in their moral courage, so that on the advent of that day, when Poland should have to call on her sons for aid, no Lithuanian should be deaf to her voice. Has she succeeded? Let the insurrection of 1831 answer the question.

The Russian Government beheld the existence of this society with a jealous eye, but the mystery, which shrouded its members, baffled all the ministerial efforts which were made to discover the names of those whom they chose to call conspirators. They wanted a pretext to have them arrested, but as the society had behaved with the greatest prudence and circumspection, the government dared not as yet make private opinion a matter of high treason. At last an incident took place which, trivial as it was, afforded a pretext for commencing that system of persecutions which, for two consecutive years, plunged in mourning almost every family in Lithuania.

On the 3rd May, 1823, the anniversary of Poland's adoption of the constitution of 1791, the students of the fifth class of the preparatory school of the university, being assembled, as usual, in their school room, one of them, Michael Plater, seized a piece of chalk and wrote on one of the boards:

Huzza for the constitution of the 3rd May! Great God! who will restore it to us?

The professor of the Russian language, who was present, denounced at once this dreadful crime to General Korsakow, then governor of Wilna, who instantly despatched a special messenger to the grand-duke Constantine with the intelligence that a revolt had broken out, but that, through the sagacious measures of the government, it had been fortunately nipped in the bud, and Count Plater, the chief of the rebels, had been arrested. The grand-duke, ever trembling with fear at the mere idea of a revolt, immediately sent Senator Nowosiltzoff to inquire into the matter.

This man seized, with avidity, an opportunity which placed in his power the means not only of materially injuring his paternal enemy, Prince Czartoryski, but also of superseding him in the presidency of Wilna; an office so richly endowed as to be an object worthy of that rapacious cupidity, which, together with inordinate ambition and lust of power, stimulated the contemptible character of this man, who saw in the possession of it nothing but the means of satisfying his sordid avarice and other evil propensities.

On his arrival at Wilna, in the full determination to find guilt in innocence, this man caused to be brought before his tribunal those who were accused of treason, when five children, the oldest of whom was hardly thirteen years of age, were brought before him. The ridicule which he was about to bring upon his sovereign by treating so seriously a mere boyish prank, did not deter him from his earnest and zealous efforts to unravel a conspiracy which never existed but in his own imagination. This course was the dictation as much of personal interest as private views. Besides, of what consequence the sacrifice of five victims, or a mother's malediction, so long as he obtained a smile of approbation from his gracious master!

Nowosiltzoff found an associate worthy of himself in the person of the professor of surgery, at the same university, named Venceslas Pelikan, who, through motives of interest, had abjured the faith of his fathers and joined the Greek Church, and who never suffered honour or reputation to stand in the way of his vile ambition. These two men persecuted the Lithuanian youth with deadly hatred.

Zan was incarcerated. Detachments of dragoons overran the country in pursuit of those who were accused. The convents of Wilna were overflowing with prisoners thus daily brought in; and banishment to Siberia was the common topic of conversation. The police agents, as well as the miserable tools of Nowosiltzoff, busied themselves in spreading rumours of horrible plots for the overthrow, not only of the throne, but also of the religion—plots newly discovered through the senator's unremitting exertions and acute patriotism. Notwithstanding all these, they were unable to adduce the least shadow of proof that could justify their persecutions.

In order to extort a confession of guilt which existed nowhere but in their own imaginations, Nowosiltzoff and Pelikan resorted to a course of most inhuman means, which the refinements of their cruelty substituted in place of the rack of the dark ages; such as the scourge while under examination, the privation of food and rest for several days, and then forcing them to feed on salt herrings, and withholding from them the means of allaying the intolerable thirst this kind of diet was intended to create.

But none of these tortures, exquisite as they were, could extort from them the avowal of a crime they had not committed, or the utterance of a single expression which could, in the least, implicate any

Senator Nowosiltzoff

of their friends. Furious at the failure of their scheme, they at last had recourse to compelling a few of their captives to sign a set of interrogatories, prepared for the occasion, and in this way succeeded in establishing something like the existence of a conspiracy, the discovery of which was to lay the foundation of their own preferment.

It was high time to put an end to this cruel farce, which had been acting now for two years. As they had totally failed in finding against the Lithuanian youth anything which could be made amenable to the ordinary tribunals, they had recourse to a plan as novel as it was outrageous.—They established a new crime or misdemeanour which they called *deraison* and made this crime to consist in these young men's attachment to, and reverence for, the usages and customs of their country, and, to this pretended crime, they awarded different degrees of punishment. (*Deraison,* such was the exact term used in the *ukase* of September, 1824. It means *opposite to reason*).

Zan was sent to the fortress of Orenbourg. Mickiewicz, and seven other Philomatians, with seven Philorathians, were dispersed in different provinces of Russia, but under the strict superintendence of the police. Michael Plater, and his classmates, who were considered his accomplices, were condemned to serve in the ranks of the Russian Army. To those who are in the habit of regarding the military service as an honourable profession, this last sentence must seem strange, but in Russia it is regarded as the most infamous punishment to which the most infamous malefactor can be condemned; and we must also add, that the condition of a Russian soldier is worse than that of a galley slave.

The iniquitous sacrifice of so many victims, which had caused a flood of innocent tears to flow, finally crowned with success the wicked wishes of Nowosiltzoff and Pelikan. The first was made Curator and the other Regent of the university. They immediately adopted a new plan of public instruction; and one can easily imagine what sort of a plan this must have been, when he is informed that Nowosiltzoff compiled it himself, and intrusted the execution of it to Pelikan.

CHAPTER 4

Projects of Marriage

The persecutions mentioned in the last chapter exasperated the public mind, and greatly increased their hatred for despotism, and schemes of vengeance were secretly planned. The Russians were detested to that degree that their individual presence could hardly be tolerated in private society. They were received in the palaces of the nobility with that distant and cold formality which could not but make them feel that, if their visits were tolerated they were not welcomed. Everything portended a revolution which, if remote, was not the less inevitable.

The inhabitants of Livonia, although personally exempt from these persecutions, yet keenly felt for the unhappy fate of their compatriots of Lithuania, and were consequently actuated by the same spirit of animosity. The cruel blow the Plater family had sustained in the arbitrary sentence which had doomed one of its members to an ignominious punishment, had greatly increased the general gloom and public sentiment. Madame Lieberg wept over the fate of her native country, once free and independent, while the young Emily, indignant at Nowosiltzoff's heinous conduct, expressed her abhorrence of the government with all the energetic frankness of a bold and noble heart, which flagrant injustice had deeply wounded.

In the meantime, the unhappy state of the country, combined with other circumstances, often brought the nobility in contact with the Russians. Lixna was situated in the vicinity of Dünabourg, and its domains, being contiguous to the grounds of the citadel, proved a source of many contentions, which compelled Madame Lieberg to have frequent intercourse with the commanding officer, and to treat him, as well as the other officers of the garrison, with some civility; and, as they were very glad to find a place of resort to dissipate the dullness and the monotony of a garrison life, they made themselves perfectly at home in their visits, which became much more frequent than was desired at Lixna.

The commanding officer of the Engineer corps, General K., was very assiduous in paying his respects to Madame Lieberg. He was a soldier and a Russian, in the full sense of the word. He had the reputation of being very clever in his profession, but extremely awkward in his manners, and so severe a disciplinarian, that he would have put himself under arrest had he accidentally discovered that he had presented himself with a button more or less on his coat than the rules and regulations prescribed.

In his visits to Lixna, General K. took particular notice of Emily, and finally resolved to marry her; the most difficult part for him, however, was how to go to work to gain the heart of the young Lithuanian, and it was no easy matter for such a lover. The heart of a young girl is not to be stormed like a fortification, and, whatever may be the skill of a soldier in the besieging of a fortress, he may find himself entirely at fault when sweet words and tender looks are the only weapons to be used; and of all others General K. was the least calculated to succeed in a love affair. He knew well how to speak to his troops of marches and battles, but with young ladies it was quite otherwise.

Whenever he found himself with Emily, he was entirely at a loss how to behave; he was awkward and almost dumb, and if he spoke at all, it was not to the purpose; he wanted words to express himself and could hardly say anything, even on the common topic of the weather. But at last, he succeeded in gaining confidence, and resolved to make, at once, a final attempt to gain his point—if not an avowal of love, at least the permission to sue for her hand, and hope for the future. He thought that no one could dare to say *no* to one who wore the epaulettes of a general and the *cordon* of St. Anne.

One day he found himself alone with Emily, and he resolved to avail himself of the opportunity. Having matured his plan and carefully selected the language he intended to use, he commenced his attack; but at the critical moment his treacherous memory failed him; yet his courage did not forsake him, and with a firm step he approached her, as if he intended to throw himself at her feet;—"*Mademoiselle*," said he, "I come to offer you my hand."

The shell was fired, the detonation made, and the general, proud of his exploit, cast his eyes down and was waiting for an answer; but seeing that none was made he resumed:

"*Mademoiselle*, I come to offer you my hand."

"Sir, I refuse it," dryly answered Emily.

He was far from expecting such an answer, and felt somewhat abashed. He did not, however, give up, but returning to the subject he continued:

"But think of my rank, Countess, and the favour which I enjoy with the Emperor."

"I am fully aware of the honour you condescend to bestow upon me by your choice, but—"

"Well—but—"

"The thing is impossible."

"Impossible!" muttered the disappointed general. "Am I so unfortunate as to have incurred your aversion?"

"I do not hate you personally."

"Is the disproportion in our ages an objection?"

"The husband should always be older than the wife."

"It is exactly what I think myself. Perhaps your heart—"

"Is perfectly free."

"You can never find a better choice."

"I do not deny it."

"Then nothing is in the way—"

"I am a daughter of *Poland*."

This last answer crushed his hopes. It was given with so much dignity, and in a tone so noble and imposing, that the general did not know what to say; he remained silent for a short time, and then left her. Having failed with the young lady, he had recourse to Madame Lieberg, whom he sought to conciliate to his views, but here he also failed. This lady assured him, that having left Emily entirely free in her choice, she should decline exercising any influence over her, and would therefore, have nothing to do in the matter.

Thus rejected, the general left Lixna in a rage, resolving never to visit it again; and, on his return to the garrison, found fault with everything and everybody, and placed several officers under arrest. He could not yet realise that it was possible for anyone to dare to refuse his hand—the hand of such a man as the commanding officer of the Engineer Corps.

"I will show them," said he, in the paroxysm of his passion, "that a Russian general can marry."

He did, indeed, marry, but not a Polish wife.

Among the officers who visited Lixna, Emily had for some time past noticed the Baron D., a Saxon by birth, and Captain of Engineers in the Russian service. He was a mild and learned man, and as much beloved by his brother officers, as he was esteemed by all that was respectable in society. She was pleased with his company; his conversation, as agreeable as it was instructive, had nothing of that pedantic affectation which is so often displayed by the learned. The Baron D., although in the vigour of his age, was nevertheless too old for Emily, who was then just entering the age of womanhood; and having seen her grow up, as it were, under his eyes, he was still in the habit of considering her as a child, and freely gave himself up to the enjoyment of a sweet friendship as pure as a virgin's mind, without even suspecting that, at some future time, she could be the object of any other sentiment.

Emily having manifested a wish to study mathematics, a science little suited to the female mind, but for which she had exhibited a decided aptitude, even from childhood, the baron offered himself as her professor; which offer being accepted, the lessons commenced.

Emily, without being perfect in beauty, was nevertheless well calculated to inspire sentiments of deep attachment; especially in a man who can value the qualities of the soul and mind, more than those of the body. She was of middle size, well-shaped, of a rather pale complexion; her face was round, with a small mouth now and then adorned with a sweet smile; she possessed a clear, sweet voice, which reached to the heart; and large blue eyes, whose brightness was softened by a melancholy expression. There was nothing very striking in her person at first sight, but, on acquaintance, one would discover new charms in her almost every day.

The baron, who, in the quality of tutor, was necessarily obliged to be with her very often, could justly appreciate her worth; and one day he was astonished at the impression she had imperceptibly made upon his heart. This discovery deeply afflicted him, and so much the more as he was well aware of the inveterate aversion Emily entertained for all that was Russian, and that he could not, therefore, dare to hope ever to succeed in obtaining her consent to the consummation of his happiness. He had the delicacy even, to abstain, most scrupulously, from any expression which could expose the state of his heart, and confining himself to the friendship of his pupil, he left the rest to time.

The heart of woman, however, instinctively becomes conscious of whatever impression her charms may have made, and it was not long before Emily perceived the feelings of her professor towards her.

It grieved her much, as she could not return the affections of the man whom she esteemed the most in the world! Love was unknown to her, and differing much in this respect from most women, she never dreamed of marriage. Poland, with whom she had identified herself, was the sole object of her thoughts. Her only ambition was to devote herself to the service of her unhappy and oppressed country. She would never have consented to destroy, by her marriage, this splendid image of her imagination; in fact, she felt that the quiet felicity of domestic life could never be her lot, and could never satisfy the ardour of her soul. But entertaining the greatest respect for the captain's feelings, as well as for his delicacy towards her, she sought to alleviate his anguish by the sincerity of her friendship.

The baron continued his lessons, and once in a while some tender expression would escape him, which, however innocent in itself, would reveal the state of his heart. To such expressions Emily never replied, and seemed not to understand them. Sometimes books and figures were laid aside for a few moments of social conversation, free, however, from anything like sentiment.

But the jealousy of General K. towards one who, though a mere admirer, had not, like him, as yet met with the mortification of a dismissal, could not allow them to enjoy this calm felicity undisturbed; for a simple captain to dare to rival him, was, as it appeared to him, an act of actual insubordination. He saw nothing but an infraction of the established order of military rank, and, in order to arrest the evil, he had recourse to his military power, by means of which he was able to impose so much duty on the baron, as to leave him but very little time to visit Lixna. His visits became less frequent and his lessons were interrupted.

At last, disgusted with these malicious persecutions, and full of indignation at such flagrant injustice, and perhaps too, in the hope of finding in absence a remedy for his unhappy attachment, the baron asked for, and obtained a transfer to the fortress of Bobruysk, where, we sincerely hope, he has found that tranquillity and peace of mind he so much required.

If ever this work should reach beyond the barrier which Russian despotism has erected against the introduction of any books in which even the name of Poland is mentioned; if ever it should happen to fall into the hands of the Baron D., he may possibly take pleasure in perusing these few pages, which, although without the honour of his personal acquaintance, we have written from Emily's recollection, who always entertained for him a sincere regard.

CHAPTER 5

Travels of Emily in Poland

The love of activity, the energy of soul, the thirst for knowledge, and the active imagination which were so glowingly portrayed in the character of our heroine, all served to inspire her with an ardent desire for travel. It was not, however, the romantic charms of foreign countries which captivated her imagination, neither had the enchanting amusements of Paris and London any attraction for her. She often said:

> Let me travel in foreign countries, to reap the fruits of a more advanced civilization than ours, to improve in sciences and industry, and return to this country with a store of useful knowledge; but, as for me, a weak and ignorant woman, all I desire is to know my own country, in order to love her still more ardently.

Accordingly, in the year 1829, the Countess Anna Plater having resolved to visit Cracow, thought she could not confer a greater pleasure on her daughter than to take her along with her. Cracow is the classic ground of Poland; everything there is purely national—the place is resplendent with the glory of our ancestors, and every spot proclaims our former power. Let us follow this young woman, and carefully note her observations. Let us observe the impression made by so many memorials on her noble and patriotic mind.

Should we exceed our prescribed limits, and, yielding to the charms of memory, unconsciously become tedious in our narrations, we sincerely hope our readers will extend their indulgence to an unfortunate exile from his beloved country, and forgive him, if, in a foreign land, that unhappy country has become the sole subject of all his dreams;—the reminiscences of home are sweet, and replete with charms for an unhappy exile.

When Emily had passed the boundaries of the Lithuanian territory, when the last Cossack sentinel had been left behind, she felt her heart relieved, as it were, from an enormous weight. It seemed to her that she breathed a purer air, and the heavens seemed to glow with brighter hues. She found herself in her cherished, though wretched kingdom. But cannot that kingdom again recover its former splendour, and reconquer its lost provinces?—Then the Russian language ceased to shock her ears, and the abhorred uniform to offend her eyes. Here all was national, and the lively peasant spoke a language she understood and loved to hear;—a great degree of happiness seemed to reign about her.

Emily had always entertained a great regard for that poor and oppressed class of people, which misery and oppression had overwhelmed; and yet this class is far more attached to its ungrateful country than those masters of theirs whom that same country has loaded with wealth and privileges. The Polish peasant cultivated the soil during peace, but when an enemy threatened his country, he mounted his swift *konic*, and flew to its defence.

★★★★★★

Konic, a small horse or pony of extreme vigour, and of an almost incredible swiftness. During the campaign of 1812, these horses, which they call *konias*, were in great demand among the French. They are common in Poland, but much more so in Lithuania.

★★★★★★

We have seen, says one of our poets, the peasant share the dangers and the glory of the country with the nobles, but never participate in their games or crimes. Proud of the performance of his duty, caring little for fame or reward, as soon as the war is over he returns to his humble cottage and resumes his ordinary occupations, rich only in the recollections which constitute the attractions and charms of his home during the long winter evenings; and while the cringing and contemptible noble bows in humble submission to the power which oppresses him, and kisses the hand that scourges him; while he eagerly seeks all that is foreign, and denies his own country, the peasant religiously adheres to the manners and customs of his ancestors, and to their hatred for the enemies of Poland.

What a vast number of precious traditions of our great men, and which would be sought for in vain elsewhere, are still in existence in almost every cottage. There the illustrious names of Pulaski, Kosciuszko, and Joseph Poniatowski still live in all their primitive splendour. The Polish language, as spoken by the peasants, possesses nothing of that sweetness and softness which is to be found in palaces and saloons. Among them, it has retained its primitive, bold, masculine roughness. In hearing it, one feels that it is the language of a people eminently warlike—one which values its independence and military valour more than anything else.

In Lithuania, where the peasant, weighed down by servitude, distrusts his master and avoids his presence; in Lithuania, where the jargon of the peasantry differs so much from the language of the nobility, Emily altogether failed in her attempts to acquire a thorough knowledge of the genuine Polish character. In Poland, however, it was quite otherwise. On her arrival in the Palatinate of Lublin, she found the genuine Pole the true type of the ancient Sarmatian. The peasant of this province is lively, industrious and frank; he is always ready to fly to the assistance of his brethren, and possesses all those characteristics which constitute a distinct and highly interesting people.

It was impossible for Emily to live among such a people and not conceive for them a high degree of esteem. She loved to converse with these people, whose singleness of heart she admired, and whose mind reflected that pure and disinterested patriotism which constituted the real strength of Poland.

She would attentively listen to, and carefully store in her memory those old traditions (to her, as the memorials of our victories and former power, full of charms,) which were the usual topics of conversation around the hearth of the cottage. Let us add, that it was among that class of people her sweet and compassionate dispositions sought out the unfortunate to console, and the needy to relieve; endeavouring to assuage, by her kindness, those sorrows which injustice and cruel prejudices had heaped upon them. She persuaded herself that to relieve the unfortunate and the destitute was, really, to serve her country.

When, on the confines of Sandomir, she asked a tall peasant, of a hold demeanour, what country he was from, he proudly answered from the *free* territory of Cracow.

The word *free* seemed to impart to him a feeling of superiority over all that surrounded him; and yet, in what does this liberty consist, of which he seemed so proud? In his having three instead of one master. But how often do we see the shadow taken for the substance, and in fact elevated to an equality with it in the eyes of the multitude!

At last she came within sight of Cracow. No pilgrim to the holy sepulchre ever hailed, with greater joy and respect the object of his veneration, than Emily did the ancient capital of her country. Cracow is the Rome of Poland, because, like Rome, it is the city of a people once free and powerful; and even now, when all around her is rotting in slavery, she seems to glory in the *name* of *free city*, which is all that remains to her of her ancient glory, and of which she seems as proud as of a shot-riddled standard just from the field of battle. One can hardly enter this city without a feeling of oppression, and in imagination, to hear the voice of the past.

Here the sacred soil contains the remains and the tomb of Krakus, the founder of the city, also the ashes of Kosciuszko, together with the monument which national enthusiasm and national gratitude have erected to the memory of this last hero of free Poland. Cracow is, as it were, the cradle and the grave of the nation. Emily felt all the emotions which the sanctity of these ruins, and the noblest recollections can awake in a truly patriotic heart. She seemed like the guardian angel of Greece, visiting the ruins of Ithaca and of Laconia at the moment when this free and powerful republic was about to reassume its rank among nations.

Alas! this Northern Greece has not been as fortunate as the country of the Hellenes. She has been obliged to resume her servitude, even as the primitive Christians were obliged by Nero to clothe themselves in tarred vestments, in order to illuminate his festivals. Emily visited the palace which not long since was the scene of so much magnificence, and which, notwithstanding all the devastations occasioned by so many wars and incendiary attempts to destroy, still retains a few traces of its former splendour.

The Vandalism of its conquerors, rather than time itself, has contributed to its destruction; the sacrilegious hand of Austria having dared even to convert the palace of our kings into common barracks. In vain did Emily look for that hall in which Jagellon once astonished all Europe by the pomp and splendour of his court. The senate chamber, like the commonwealth it represented, no longer existed; all that here and there offered itself to her view, were a few sepulchral fragments, and some remains of paintings in the Gothic windows, standing as if in astonishment at their survival of all that formerly surrounded them, and the meaning of which the mind laboured in vain to explain.

Broken hearted at the aspect of these sad ruins, Emily sought refuge in the vaults of the cathedral, where the sacred ashes of our kings and of our illustrious men are reposing. When alone, in the midst of ages passed, she evoked, from their tombs, the shades of the Batorys and the Sobieskis; passed centuries rose before her, and in her ardent imagination, everything before her in the mansion of the dead, assumed a new life. It was there the Tzar of Moscow sought the protection of the holy Father against the sword of Batory,—it was there the Austrian ambassador threw himself at the feet of Sobieski, exclaiming: "Oh! Sire, save Christianity." All these recollections nearly overpowered the feelings of our heroine; and here she would have remained all her life, or, rather until the shout of independence should ring from the Niemen to the Vistula, calling for men and arms to expel the common oppressor.

On her return thence, Emily met the Austrian Commissary, who then resided in the vicinity of Cracow. He seemed to her the spectre of slavery itself, who, on her awakening from her dreams of liberty, had come to seize her. At the sight of him, she felt a great oppression at the heart, and she turned from him with horror.

Cracow is one of the handsomest, as well as one of the largest cities in Poland, and its environs are delightful. Seldom does anything finer or more picturesque meet the eye.—Here you meet with opulent boroughs and comfortable villages, the habitations of cheerful and happy country people; and there, one is delighted with the smiling prospects of rich valleys, commanded by beautiful knolls, the site of elegant mansions, once the abode of abundance, felicity and hilarity; but now, of wretchedness, solitude and degradation.

The Carpathian mountains, with their hoary summits, seem to form, in their remoteness, a suitable back-ground to this grand picture, forming, as a whole, a spectacle ever to be admired. Emily also visited the charming valley of Prondnik, and obtained a stalactite from the cave called to this day the Royal Grotto, because in former times, Ladislas (le-bref) occupied it as the only retreat he could find against the close pursuit of his enemies.

In her visits to the spacious halls of the Piaskowa Skala, a painting representing a beautiful black-eyed young nun, with a sword in her hand, attracted her particular attention, and, excited by curiosity, she sought for an explanation, which the keeper of the castle afforded. He said it was the portrait of a lady of the Wielopolski family, who lived a great many years since, and who, imbued from infancy with the spirit of chivalry, disguised herself in man's attire and joined the army against the foes of her country. She became celebrated for her bravery and heroic achievements, but no one ever suspected that the valiant arm, which so skilfully wielded the sword, was, by nature, destined to handle only the distaff.

Mere chance did unravel the mystery. The heroine cast off her military trappings, and anxious of shunning a world which could not forgive her so glaring a departure from its received customs, sought the seclusion of a cloister. But habituated as she was to the fatigues of the camp, she could not endure the monotonous tranquillity of a contemplative life, and she soon after died. But, as a memorial of her bold adventure, she was buried with her arms, and with them also did the painter represent her.

These incidents threw Emily into a deep meditation, and we may well say that the keeper's narrative had a decided influence on her subsequent life; and under the tent as well as on the field of battle the image of the nun of Piaskowa Skala was ever present to her mind. She often made it the subject of her conversation, and that painting remained indelibly impressed on her memory. Much to her regret, she could not learn from the keeper either the name of the war in which she served, or the time of her death.

From Cracow she repaired to the capital of the kingdom. On her route she visited the famous field of Raszyn, where Prince Joseph Poniatowski, with eight thousand Polish recruits, fought in 1809, against forty thousand Austrians. But Warsaw, with all its pomp, its palaces and theatres, could not satisfy a soul in which strong emotions had become a passion. She seemed actually wrapt in the past, and in it she thought to descry a pledge for the future.

All the amusements of the capital, on the grave as it were of her country's freedom, she regarded as actually criminal, and, if at any time, she was allured by the hilarity and pleasures of the day, a Russian presence would soon dissipate the delusion, and she would at once relapse into her habitual melancholy. The *Tzarevitsch*—a tiger in human shape, had selected this city for his lair, and the pestiferous breath of the police, contaminated its atmosphere. The sight of her young countrymen, who, under a Russian commander, were daily drilled in the public square, filled Emily's heart with anguish.

She reflected that in these young warriors consisted all the strength of her country, and fain would she see the day when they would use their talents, and turn their arms against their country's oppressors. One year after, they did most worthily realise the most sanguine wishes of this patriotic young maiden; and this little army surpassed even the hope the Poles had placed in their forces.

Meanwhile, if Warsaw, this second capital of the ancient republic, does not possess' the importance of Cracow, yet there are many glorious recollections connected with her which must cause emotions in a Polish heart, and which did not fail to exercise great influence on our young traveller's mind and imagination.

It was Sigismond III. who transferred the seat of government from Cracow to Warsaw; and the last king, Stanislas Augustus, even obtained permission from the States in Session, to be crowned in this city. The first object which attracted Emily's attention, was the royal palace, situated on a lofty elevation, which commands a fine view of the Vistula and its opposite bank; she admired its two Halls of Assembly. There she recalled to her mind the assembly of 1773, as much disgraced by the ignominious conduct of Poninski, as it was rendered illustrious by the patriotism of Reyten.

She paused with respect, on the threshold which had served as a pillow to this eminent citizen, when he protested against the most revolting of tyrannies. It was in this hall the voice of our fathers resounded on the memorable third of May, 1791, and also the 28th June, 1812, when the General Confederation of Poland was organising. She, after this, traversed the great hall composed of marble, and ornamented with all that architecture and gilt bronze can offer in richness and elegance. She also visited the hall of reception, decorated with six large paintings, by Bacciarelli, representing the most remarkable epochs in Polish history, and also with twenty-two busts, in black marble, of illustrious characters of the country.

From the palace, she entered the cathedral, knelt at the foot of the altar, and rehearsed in her soul the many *Tè Deums* and other songs of joy and thanksgiving which had resounded under its vaults, in the celebration of the victories of our ancestors. It was there the victory of Kluzyn, won by Zolkiewski, that of Kircholm, by Chodkiewicz, as well as those of Chocim and of Vienna, by Sobieski, were celebrated. But the object which she was most anxious to visit, was the ruin of the Moscovite chapel. Under its vaults were reposing the ashes of those *Tzars* of Moscow, whom the illustrious Zolkiewski had brought thither in 1611 as prisoners of war, and having died at Gostynin, their remains were there deposited.

In the year 1634, King Vladislas IV. having concluded a treaty of peace with Moscow, in consequence of a request on the part of the

Tzars, gave up the ashes of Tchouisky. Under the reign of Stanislas Augustus, Catharine II. having succeeded to the throne of the *Tzars*, after having placed on the throne of Poland an old favourite of hers, gave positive orders to her ambassador, Repnine, to cause the marble tablets, which bore the records of their former disaster, to be broken in pieces. And yet, what remained of these ancient monuments were too offensive to the Russian Government.

Alexander and Catharine hastened to demolish the last remaining monuments of our power, as well as of their ancestor's weakness; as if this act of Vandalism could obliterate the memory of these events, or tear a glorious page from our history. What a melancholy contrast in this very capital, where two centuries ago the sovereigns of Moscow were chained to the triumphal cars of our brave Zolkiewski, and where now, in this same capital, a Russian potentate wields the supreme power! This barbarous nation now treats Poland as a conquered country. The time has gone by when she thought herself but too happy to be able to obtain, for her sovereign, a son of the king of Poland.

She afterwards visited the historical plains of Wola Powonzki the *Pere-la-chaise* of Poland. She also visited the places which were the scene of the seizure and carrying off of Stanislas Augustus. Her soul was filled with indignation. She could not forgive to Kuzma the preservation of Catharine's vile instrument,—the author or the witness of the dismemberment and overthrow of our ancient republic.

Praga also received the tribute of Emily's tears. Praga, the suburb of Warsaw, is one of the most hallowed places in Poland, and it is one which Sowarow inundated with blood; on the scene of this bloody tragedy did she offer her humble prayers to the Supreme Judge of the universe for the eternal peace of Jazinski and his brave companions; and at the same time, she implored a just and retributive vengeance upon their murderers.

Emily did not sojourn long in Warsaw. No one ever passed through Poland without visiting Pulaway—a most delightful location and magnificently embellished by art. The treasures of science were amassed in profusion in this truly great and royal place. All was charming, all was attractive to the curious, travelling for instruction as well as amusement. And what is it now? Nothing but a heap of ruins. A civilized foe would, at least, have spared a place hallowed by so many recollections; but all this was an additional incentive to destroy and to overwhelm with horrors. It was even a grandson who gave the order to fire on the palace of his ancestor;—it was the Duke of Würtemberg who ravaged the dominions of the princess Czartoryska.

Besides the beauties of nature and of art which invited the traveller to visit Pulaway, this place possessed a further attraction, which, for a Pole, was a purely national one. In this place, the enlightened patriotism of its owners had carefully collected the several historical fragments, and all the traditions of our ancient Poland; and had preserved in this Temple of the Sybil, the precious remains of our ancestors. In that Polish Westminster reposed, side by side, the protective arm of the warrior and the enlightened head of the scholar. There, one might see the bones of Boleslas the Great, and the ashes of Kopernik; the sword of Ladislas-le-Bref, who by extraordinary firmness in misfortunes, his intrepidity in battle, and his clemency on the throne, saved Poland, and made her formidable to her enemies.

The plain writing table of his son and successor, whose greatest ambition it was to deserve the title of king to his people, and on whom a grateful posterity conferred the name of Casimir the Great; the stand of colours, the embroidery of which was the work of Hedwige's own hands, and perhaps the very one under which she rallied the warriors of Poland and led them on to victory; some monuments of Sigismond I., a contemporary and the equal of Charles V.; his son's portfolio, containing the portraits of his beloved sister Isabella of Hungary, and of his adored wife; that of the young and interesting Barbara Radziwill, who found in her exalted rank nothing but misfortune, and, at last, a premature death; the sword of Batory, alas! too soon lost to Poland; relics of the great Zamoyski; the baton of command of the valiant Czarnecki, the trophies won from the infidels by Sobieski, who, although a great warrior, was nevertheless a bad king; who covered Poland with immortal honour, yet hastened its ruin; all these were collected at Pulaway and arranged in the greatest order—offering to Poland's children living testimonies of what their ancestors once had been.

They spoke the language of the soul, and no one, unless destitute of patriotism and generous sentiments, could look at them without emotion. Then came another series of relics of more modern, but no less glorious times—the relics of suffering Poland, which has been fighting for more than fifty years, in order to regain her independence.

The constitution of the 3rd of May, the confederation of Bar, and the wars of Bonaparte, had furnished the Temple of the Sybil with a great many new objects which the Poles held in great veneration, and which they sometimes wept over. All these great events were there typified and recalled to the memory by sacred relics.

There, also, might be seen the ivory and ebony vases, the construction of which beguiled the tediousness of Kosciuszko's long captivity, and more than one lance had found admission into this sacred depository for having sustained the splendour of the Polish name, even at a time when Poland might have been sought for in vain on the map of the world.

The Temple of the Sybil, although a large and spacious building, was nevertheless found too small to contain all the trophies of our ancient power, and display at the same time those of a more recent date. The owner of Pulaway was obliged to add to it a Gothic building, which recalled to mind many recollections of other nations, besides those of Poland. Who can read the inscription, which stood above the portico, without a hearty response to the wish expressed by it? Where is the Pole, who has not oftentimes, from the bottom of his heart and with solemnity, repeated these words:

May one day, our victories obliterate even the remembrance of our misfortunes!

Those whom our reverses had discouraged, and even induced to despair of their country's cause, would come to Pulaway to restore their sinking courage.

Those even who, inured to servitude, had unhappily forgotten their country's rights, would return from this holy pilgrimage ready to sacrifice, not only the peace of their home, but life itself, for the salvation of Poland. We can hardly tell what impression all these produced upon the mind of Emily, whose wishes and designs all concentred in the recovery of Poland's liberty and former glory.

Emily returned to Lithuania more of a Pole than ever. Her character assumed a stronger cast, less subject to fears, and more masculine; but, at the same time, a melancholy sadness took possession of her mind, and developed in her that pensive, yet seductive grace, which never afterwards deserted her; the religious principle, which had been early instilled into her, took still stronger root in her mind. Before her journey, she would, sometimes, mingle with her companions in their several amusements; but now, she avoided the joyous dance, and shunned every kind of society which was not in sympathy with her own feelings.

She often passed whole days in solitude, with no other company than what her own thoughts and reveries afforded her. And what pleasures could the present offer to one who lived only with the past? How could she descend to the level of men who patiently and quietly submitted to the yoke; she, who was yet full of the recollections gathered in Poland, and of new hopes which were budding in her soul?

CHAPTER 6

Death of the Mother of Emily

The year 1830 brought with it, to the tender and affectionate Emily, a heavy affliction, in the loss of the deeply cherished object of all her earthly affections. Overcome by misfortune, rather than age, her mother was taken dangerously ill. Country, ambition, and dreams of glory were all forgotten, by Emily, as soon as she perceived her mother's life to be in danger. During her whole illness, Emily never left her mother's sick bed for an instant. Day and night, seated at the head of her bed, she watched the slightest of her movements, and endeavoured to anticipate the least of her wishes, and would not, during the whole time, allow herself any rest.

The poignancy of her grief increased as the symptoms became less favourable; but she endeavoured to suppress her sobs so as not to alarm her dying mother. In vain did several of the family, apprehensive of losing the daughter as well as the mother, endeavour to prevail upon her to take some rest:—"Who, better than a daughter, can attend a sick mother?" would be her reply, absolutely declining, at the same time, their kind offices. And when, almost dragged away by force, she left her post for a few minutes, her mother was pictured to her, in imagination, in the grasp of death for want of necessary attention; she immediately returned in haste to the chamber, to calm her fears at the bed of sorrow, from which nothing could afterwards induce her to absent herself, even for an instant.

Notwithstanding the unremitting care of her daughter, Madame Plater, at length, sunk under her protracted illness. She was highly respected for her nobleness of character, and her many virtues. The sport of fortune, from her infancy, she had little desire to remain in a world, which had afforded her so few happy days. Her only regret, in quitting it, was to leave her daughter's happiness in such a state of

45

uncertainty. With her dying breath, she consigned her poor orphan to the maternal care of Madame Lieberg. She conjured her to watch over Emily as her own daughter. She then blessed her, and gave up her pure spirit, while yet in the act of invoking the Supreme Father of the orphan in behalf of her daughter.

Weak minds alone sink under the weight of their grief, and seek relief in tears; while a strong mind will repress it, without subjecting itself even to the suspicion of insensibility; such grief is the more consuming as it is altogether internal. Emily manifested but few signs of grief at the death of her mother, but a deep sorrow was undermining her health. But religion came to her aid in this emergency. In confronting death, nothing can be more comforting, or have a more powerful effect, than the sentiment which directs our thoughts to a better life, beyond the grave.

Perfectly resigned, and repressing every mark of sorrow, she in person superintended the funeral obsequies, determined that nothing should be wanting in these august solemnities; and shortly after caused a modest monument to be erected over that grave which contained her earthly treasure. To this spot would she every day repair, to sprinkle it with fresh flowers, and address her humble prayer to heaven for the eternal peace of her mother. This sad event entirely crushed her spirit, and the wound which it inflicted was never completely healed, but bled afresh at the slightest recollection of it.

Several months afterwards, Emily, in the midst of the din of the camp, entirely devoted to her country, seemed to live but for Poland. But when her mind recurred to her mother, she would seek to meditate in solitude, if possible, for the rest of the day.

From the moment of her mother's death, Emily felt that her heart was nothing but a vast desert. Possessed of an affectionate disposition, she felt the need of some object upon which she might fix her affections. She addressed herself to her father, whom she scarcely knew, and who had been separated from her mother in early life, and had lived far away from his family, without cultivating with them the slightest intercourse.

She, for some time previous, had devoted to his own use all the small savings her means and position in society would permit her to lay up. Now, that she had the sole control of her destiny, she wished to be near him. She, at times, fancied him suffering on a bed of sickness, without anyone to console him, and entirely abandoned to the precarious attendance of strangers. She would have looked upon herself as criminal, had she hesitated longer; she therefore left Lixna for Lithuania. She used her best endeavour to obtain an interview, but without the least success. She had the affliction of seeing all her advances repelled. She ought certainly to have renounced, at once, her favourite hope of devoting her days, as well as her fortune, to the welfare of her father, but no;—she interested in her favourite plan several friends of the family, and retired to the residence of one of her aunts, at Antuzow, to await the result of her efforts.

It was at this place the news of the insurrection of 1830 reached her, to invite her to more glorious undertakings.

Her moral sufferings had impaired her health. Sea-bathing was prescribed, and she repaired to Libau. The city of Libau (Lipawa) is situated on the coast of the Baltic, in Courland, and is much frequented by the Lithuanians, the Samogitians, and the Livonians. During the fine season, sea-bathing is productive of excellent effects on the health of its visitors. On one of those beautiful days, common to that climate, the visitors at Libau formed a party for a sea excursion. Among many other officers of the Russian Army, was Gen. K., a native of Courland. The freedom and mutual confidence which generally prevailed on su.ch occasions, led him to allude to, or rather indiscreetly reveal, a piece of information which, till that time, he had kept a profound secret. He produced French letters and French journals, which furnished a minute account of the memorable scenes of July.

Emily Plater felt the importance of them, and thought she foresaw, in this event, the future liberation of her country. This news remained engraved upon her mind and heart, and knowing the proofs of courage displayed by the Parisians, they received her full admiration. From this moment, she eagerly embraced politics. All that she could learn in respect to the Belgian revolution, as well as the popular movements in other countries of Europe, raised her spirits to the highest pitch. On the future destiny of Poland, concentrated all her ideas; and the energies of her mind full well informed her, that she could not remain indifferent to the new destiny of her glorious country.

Here ends the private life of Emily Plater; and as such it is the life of a woman scarcely known, passed in peace and retirement, and leaving no remembrance but in the hearts of a few friends, and the casual recollections of her neighbours. But from this time, she belongs to history, which will bear an impartial record of her glorious deeds during our late revolution. But, before entering upon this second epoch of her life, which is by far the most brilliant, and which is the particular object of our labours, I feel that I ought to furnish a faithful portrait of her, simply as a woman; and I cannot do this better than by permitting her cousin, and earliest friend, to present her views of Emily's character in her own language. The following is a letter sent to me by Mademoiselle D———, in answer to one of my own addressed to her, requesting some particulars respecting Emily's early life and character.

"She would never act like other young persons of her own sex, their games and amusements having no attractions for her. She detested balls and fine dress. She always selected for the colour of her dress, when the choice was left to her, a dark colour and generally black. Emily was naturally timid, but she knew how to conquer this timidity.

"When engaged in riding, she took pride in her falls, and would remount her steed to brave new dangers, and afterwards spoke of such incidents with great satisfaction. Her favourite amusements were to wander in a sledge in the woods or over the ice of the Dzwina, in quest of imaginary dangers, and to shoot at a mark. Her writing table was not covered with the elegant trifles which usually surround young persons, but with mathematical books and instruments. She also had several works on celebrated women of all ages, which she perused and reperused with the greatest enthusiasm.

"Her closet was adorned with the portraits of Joan d'Arc, of Poniatowski, of Kosciuszko, and Bobelina. Notwithstanding her ardent admiration of all that is great and glorious, she possessed an excessive sensibility, the expression of which she always avoided, lest it should detract from her love of glory.

"She must have been well aware that her father had never appreciated the merits of her mother; nevertheless, she loved him, and transmitted to him her small income, although she never had received from him the slightest mark of attachment. She was the joy and solace of her mother, whom she loved with the fullest affection. For children, as well as the poor, she always felt a deep interest.

"Although she repressed every exhibition of tenderness of feeling, and would have preferred the appearance of insensibility to that of weakness, yet she was compassionate, and no one more sincerely sympathized with the afflictions or the prosperity of those who possessed her affections. Free from selfishness, her heart was suspicious to such a degree, that her distrust surpassed, if possible, the deception of the generality of mankind; at the same time, her open frankness could not have been surpassed: never has the least dissimulation tarnished her character. She was so lofty in her thoughts that her ideas were, sometimes, mistaken for egotism. Often has her candour brought upon her the ill will of many, for she was brief and even rude, to those who were disagreeable to her. Although aware of this feeling, if it may be so called, she either could not, or would not conquer it.

"Having very little taste for the society of those of her own age, she formed an intimate acquaintance with one of her neighbours who was her senior. She would patiently listen to advice dictated by experience, not however to follow it implicitly, but in order to be able the better to discuss the difference of opinions. Not only would she never be offended when told of her faults, but would insist on being informed of such as might be discovered in her conduct. If she ever excused any fault in herself, it was only to prove that it had been committed unintentionally.

"Her temper was naturally variable; she might, therefore, have been inclined to gayety. But she would have subdued this propensity, even if she had possessed it, as unworthy that gravity which she thought more suitable to that vague futurity, which was the subject of her reveries, without offering any definite object to her wishes.

"Although she believed her heart incapable of love, yet her conduct was influenced by an instinctive prudence, which would never allow her to forget her duty. Had she ever married, no view to ambition, neither birth nor fortune, would have in the least, determined her choice. The disinterested inclination of her own heart would have been her only guide, and she would have loved with the deepest passion.

"The attention of young people is generally directed to objects of luxury, dress and fashion; but with Emily it was not so. Scarcely anything but arms ever engaged her serious attention. Her pistols always lay upon her writing-table, and she took care of her own horse. Although of delicate constitution naturally, she never spared it, being in the hope of inuring it to toil and labour.

"Although possessing all the sensibility of her sex, with an unbounded devotedness to the few individuals for whom she felt any attachment, she was never subject to the capricious fancy of her sex. She was ever ready to give proof of her attachment, even at the risk of incurring the censure of public opinion, which, by the way, she little cared for, as the only guide she ever followed was her conscience. The most glorious event of our time has developed all the energy of a character which no domestic felicity could ever have satisfied.

"She possessed great knowledge of human nature, which she was fond of studying and thoroughly examining. She took particular delight in unveiling, as it were, the mysteries of the soul, and analysing man, and ascertaining the *primum mobile* of his actions. She wished to raise that vail, behind which egotism and meanness are wont to screen themselves; and she was astonished to find how small the number who could stand such a test without losing much in her estimation."

CHAPTER 7

Revolution of the 29th of November

A revolution was about to break out in Poland. The indefatigable labours of the Patriotic Association, as well as the inveterate hatred the Poles have always fostered for their oppressors, rendered this revolution unavoidable, and the French revolution of July accelerated the event.

On the fall of Napoleon, the Dutchy of Warsaw, like an apple of discord, was, as it were, thrown amongst the kings who were all anxious to share the spoils of the great conqueror. Prussia and Austria asserted the priority of their claims—claims having only rapine and violence for their foundation.

Russia, whose favourite plan it is to enlarge her European possessions, availed herself of the advantage of actual occupation, and appeared, by no means, willing to relinquish her prey. Diplomatic agency was in full activity, and unable to conciliate so many clashing claims, adopted a middle course, and yielded to the demands of the cabinet of St. Petersburg. But in this very concession were the germs of future difficulties, which were to obstruct the course of her ambition, and place her in a position absolutely false.

The Congress of Vienna, in the plenitude of its wisdom, decreed that Poland should be erected into a kingdom, whose crown was to adorn the head of the Emperor of Russia, and should have a constitutional form of government, under a sovereign who never knew any other law, all over his vast empire, but his own will, and who, in the title of king of Poland, saw merely a single addition to the long list of his numerous sovereignties. This is the same kingdom which the mean policy of the European cabinets recognise, at this day, as a legal one, and in behalf of which they have ventured to submit a few feeble and humble remonstrances; as if a congress of all the kings of Europe had the right to sanction an act which the people, not only would not sanction, but also would reject with indignation.

The Poles, conquered with Napoleon, in submitting to the decision of the conquerors, earnestly protested against this iniquitous act of the Holy Alliance. They had not made, since 1795, so many sacrifices, they had not lavished, for a period of twenty years, so much blood and treasure, and all for the mere shadow of a country destitute of political existence, a real slavery under the specious vail of liberty—a liberty as precarious as illusory, and wholly subject to the caprices of a despot. Patriotic associations were everywhere organised, and preparations made to resist this persecution; it was these associations which, at a later period, brought about the revolution of the 29th of November.

The first idea of these associations is due to Dombrowski. This veteran of our liberty, who had brought off the remains of the white eagle, and thus prolonged the existence of the Polish nation, under the tents of the fraternal French, groaned at the condition of a country which he had imagined free, powerful and glorious. He saw with grief that it was in vain to reckon upon the help of other people, or to intrust the safety of the country to the selfish policy of foreigners.— Napoleon, who set up as many kingdoms as he had brothers, what had he done for Poland, in return for the blood of two hundred thousand Poles, who had perished in the service of France?

And, as to the kingdom which he had erected, where was the guarantee for the permanence of its existence and institutions? Who could assure us from day to day that the capricious will of this master would not violate, or abolish, even that constitution which he deigned to bestow upon us, the better to entrap and destroy us? Having nothing, therefore, either to hope or to fear from others, it was necessary to turn to the advantage of the nation that valour which had contributed, for so long a time, to the glory and power of foreigners. The ancient energies of Poland must be aroused, which, in order to be strong and powerful, needed but to have confidence in its own strength. The dying flame of patriotism must be revived in all hearts, in order that Poland may, one day, recover for itself its lost power.

Such were the patriotic sentiments of the good and virtuous Dombrowski in 1818. Intrusted to a few patriotic friends, they did not fall into a barren soil, and soon the national freemasonry hastened to carry into effect these ideas, and it brought a strong hand to the work.

The association was organised upon a vast and powerful plan, secretly pervading the whole country, and numbering, among its members, all that was noble and patriotic in the land; its ramifications, in the invaded provinces, were numerous, and it had at its disposal, not only the moral and physical strength of the whole people, but also a vast capital, which the devotedness of the members of this association had taken care to provide. The nobility overcoming ancient prejudices, and trampling, as it were, upon its own privileges, entered commerce, and thus prepared the way for that desirable state of equality between the two great classes of the community, the nobles and the plebeians, which, notwithstanding, are still kept asunder in Poland by a strong line of demarcation.

The national spirit was roused, the fire of patriotism was enkindled in all hearts, and the country, undermined in every direction, was insensibly preparing itself for the great work of its political regeneration. Arms were prepared; at the appointed hour, everyone was to be at his post, and Poland was to regain its freedom.

On the other hand the Emperor Alexander, but too soon realising the fears of the brave Dombrowski, hastened to declare open war against free institutions, and commenced by violating the constitution of the kingdom. The destruction of the freedom of the press, the establishment of the censorship, arbitrary banishment, the erecting of special tribunals for the trial of all cases between citizens and the government, taxes laid upon the nation by simple ordinances, all signalized the march of absolutism. The *diet* of 1820 energetically protested against these flagrant violations of the charter, and strongly and vigorously opposed these new outrages of a perjured government.

But Alexander knew how to rid himself of an obstinate and intractable chamber, and this legal opposition served but to irritate the Autocrat, who had been accustomed to a blind obedience on the part of his Russian subjects. He even thought, at one time, of annihilating the constitutional kingdom, which was a great obstacle to him in the exercise of his power; and, in order to sound the people, he caused to be published, in 1821, a rescript, in which, after having made an expose of the bad state of the Polish finances, he proceeded to say:

That the time had at last arrived, when it must be decided whether the kingdom could support itself by its own resources, or whether it ought not, after having come to a consciousness of its lack of means in this respect, to submit to an established order of things better conformed to its limited resources.

A general cry of indignation Convinced him that his project would have met with a very powerful resistance, and that the time for striking a decided blow had not yet arrived.

Besides, Alexander as a crafty and expert politician, knew precisely when to stop, and in battering down the liberties of Poland, he would carefully avoid any act, which could possibly alarm the nation and reduce her to a state of despair. During his life, therefore, the patriotic associations merely took measures to repel, openly, the attacks of despotism, but were ever on the watch for more favourable circumstances to unfurl the standard of freedom; and this policy was the more necessary, as, on account of the peace generally prevailing throughout the earth during the latter part of the reign of this monarch, he would have been enabled to bring the whole weight of his power upon Poland, and thereby crush her by an overwhelming force.

Moreover, the Polish patriotic society thought it best to await the result of the operations of the patriotic society of slaves in the interior of Russia, with which society they considered their own connected by the ties of a common interest. For even in the interior of Russia, ardent minds, inimical to despotism, were engaged in secret movements; there, even, conspiracies were forming, and even in the bosom of the most hideous slavery, the most shameful barbarity, plots were weaving in favour of the liberty of the people and the well-being of the nation.

The excursion made by the Russians into France, on the downfall of Napoleon, and their long sojourn there, were not without benefit to them. Seeing, in this country, the people happy and free, in the enjoyment of their rights, and governed by laws which were humane, wise and reasonable, they envied these blessings of civilization, and wished to transfer them into their own country, where the state of slavery and misery were truly revolting to them, when compared with the state of prosperity enjoyed by other nations. In the first place, they united their efforts for the melioration of the agricultural and industrial classes; this is evident from the title of the society which bore the name of the *Benevolent Society*, or that of the *Green Book*.

But a more profound knowledge of their country, and of the obstacles which were opposed to them, soon convinced them that the root of the evil was in the vicious constitution of the monarchy itself; and that, without that liberty which was the vital principle of a people, no scheme of amelioration would be practicable. They, therefore, extended their views, and resolved to break the rusty sceptre of absolutism, and bestow upon Russia a constitution, formed upon the model of the fullest natural and individual liberty.

The principal strength of the reigning family lay in the army, which was reduced to a state of blind subordination, and the chief officers of which, for the most part foreigners and without country, were influenced by no higher motive than that of serving him who paid them best. The liberals of Russia then sought, by every possible means, to utterly destroy, or at least to render useless, the chief support of the reigning family; and for this purpose, as the surest and most effectual means, they undertook to form a strong body of partisans, in the very bosom of the army, and in this they succeeded. Soon there existed two great associations, which were organised, one in the southern, the other in the northern, part of the empire; both were bound by the same oath and had in view the same end.

Col. Pestel, chief of the southern society, found himself, by his position, brought into close contact with the former Polish provinces, and was not slow in effecting communication with the patriots of the country. Acknowledging the flagrant injustice done to Poland, he promised to restore to it all the provinces which were not yet *Russified,* (Pestel's own expression); and the Poles, on their part, agreed to act in concert with him, and to aid the Russian liberals, at the proper moment, in the great work of the regeneration of the immense empire of the *Czars.* The revolution, embracing a vast plan, was in one day to embrace all Russia, and to render her free, almost in spite of herself.

A traitor, unfortunately, insinuated himself into their ranks. He denounced to the emperor the secret designs of the society, and gave him a complete list of the conspirators. Amazed at the gigantic strides of liberal opinions, and at the great projects in agitation, together with the powerful means possessed for carrying them into effect, the *Czar* did not dare, at first, to make an open and direct attack upon the conspiracy, which extended its ramifications into the most distant provinces of his vast empire. His timid and wavering disposition would not admit of bold decision; a powerful blow was with him impossible. He was not the man to conquer the enemy by prompt action and at a single blow.

Relying, then, on the craftiness of his policy, he limited himself to neutralizing the influence of the accused, a list of which he carefully kept in his portfolio; to this end he, under various pretexts, deprived them of the command of the troops, and confided it to the hands of his trusty friends, on whom he was perfectly sure he could rely.

Alexander died. Nicholas was about to take possession of the power which Constantine had relinquished, some years before, for the purpose of effecting a marriage with Jean Grudzinska. This was the favourable moment for action. The new emperor must be hurled from the throne, before firmly seated upon it; or rather he must not be permitted to mount it at all. So favourable an occasion would not, for a long time, again present itself, and it was resolved to profit by it.

The liberals of St. Petersburg commenced the attack, and thus gave the signal for the rest. But, unhappily, they placed, by far, too great reliance upon the mass of the people, who were not yet sufficiently advanced in civilization to feel the need or the value of liberty. Riléieff was also guilty of an unpardonable fault, in hastening the explosion without previously giving the chief of the southern society information of it. Consequently, the revolution, instead of being general, was only in part, and thus furnished the Emperor Nicholas the means of suppressing it in detail.

The *emeute*, the rebellion, for so an unsuccessful revolution is termed, the *emeute* of St. Petersburg having thus miscarried, the arrest of all the liberals became an easy matter, and they were prosecuted with the utmost rigor, under the firm resolution of not permitting a single one to escape. It was a pestilence of which the soil of the empire must be thoroughly purged, inasmuch as it was of a contagious character. The judicial investigations proved that they were connected with the Polish patriots, and the order was issued to pursue the patriotic society.

In the execution of this order, more than two hundred persons were arrested in Poland. A special commission, composed of Russians and Poles, commenced their inquiries. But whether the secret had been religiously kept by the accused, or that the connections of the Russian liberals did not extend to the kingdom of Poland, but were limited to the invaded provinces; true it is the commission found no trace of a plot, and in its report to the emperor, contented itself with denouncing, in vague terms, the existence of a secret society, organised without the consent or knowledge of the police. This report incensed Nicholas, who really wished to seize upon the guilty, for the mere gratification of punishing them. He blamed the commission, and sent eight of the principal ones accused to the tribunal of the Diet, the only court having jurisdiction over crimes of state.

Nicholas, however, deceived himself, in his expectation of finding in the supreme court of the kingdom, men base enough to become the tools of his vengeance, or weak enough to be intimidated by his power. Notwithstanding the organisation of this tribunal, and the mode of its proceedings, were the work of his arbitrary power; notwithstanding, too, the censure cast upon the preceding commission, and intimations, by other means, clearly showed what was the wish of the emperor, out of forty members composing the tribunal, only one proved himself unworthy of the name he disgraced. All the others, including their venerable president Bielinski, declared the accused not guilty.

Constantine, highly incensed, arrested the publication of the judgment; and it was not until after a delay of six months that Nicholas ordered it to be put in execution, accompanying his order with the expression of his severe disapprobation of the conduct of the highest national court, excepting from his censure, only *one*—the base and infamous traitor, Krasinski, who alone had pronounced the accused guilty.

The deplorable end of the Russian liberals, and the persecutions which for three years threatened the members of the patriotic society in Poland, disorganised their plans, and occasioned a delay of the revolution.

Notwithstanding, far from being cast down by these persecutions, the associates again united, and applied themselves with still greater zeal for the accomplishment of the grand work; they, however, endeavoured to be more on their guard, and to enshroud their movements in still greater secrecy. In the meantime, nothing appeared to favour their efforts in the political world; and Europe, involved in lethargy, seemed to offer them no point of support. There was no star, in their horizon, which could serve them as a guide in their march to independence, and all the forces the nation could possibly muster, were insufficient to act against the innumerable masses of all the Russias.

Austria and Prussia, as parties to the dismemberment of Poland, were too much interested in the utter annihilation of its nationality, ever to consent to favour the operations of the patriots. England, exhausted by her long wars against Napoleon, was taking her rest, after a victory which had loaded her with opprobrium and enormous debts. France, weary of glory, was also reposing after her long and terrible convulsions, her numerous battles and her brilliant victories; and under the shade of a new throne. Since 1815, she had exhibited but one single sign of life, and that was to crush, in Spain, the liberty which had once more raised its head there; and, moreover, France is too distant.

The popular associations, repressed as they had been by the blighting influence of despotism, with the exception of those who were fortunate enough to escape the vigilance of this Holy Alliance of kings, were nearly all destroyed. They moved only in the night, in secret whispers, and far from the observation of the police, or of traitors. All Europe trembled in presence of the Autocrat of the North. The Polish patriots, therefore, had to rely entirely on their own resources, and far from recoiling at dangers so apparent, they did not despair of overcoming all these obstacles, and of recovering their independence, which had been so violently wrested from them.

But some important events supervened, and a few months of political storms and glorious movements almost entirely changed the face of Europe.

The cholera and the Turkish war had decimated that formidable army, the enormous mass of which had caused the scale to incline in favour of Russia. The French people had risen, as great, as brave, and as victorious as in former times. The hydra of the Holy Alliance had been made to tremble, and the people, raising a lengthened cry of joy, had proved to the world that they were conscious of their own strength, and that they could still perform great deeds. The three great days of France were the torch thrown into the midst of Europe, which was waiting in silence the signal.

The French is the eldest of all the nations; it guides the march of humanity in these modern times; it has only to impart the impulse, and the others follow their example. The signal, so long, and so impatiently expected, was given—the list was open and waiting for the parties—champions were by no means wanting. This same people, who had first raised the standard of liberty and called on other nations to rally around it, relapsed into its former apathy, and stopped short in the midst of its triumph. But who could have foreseen such a thing? All was fire and enthusiasm, and loud in the cry for liberty; and the cry resounded through Europe, which, undermined as it were in her foundations, experienced, to her very centre, the most terrible convulsions. Thrones tottered at their bases, and kings were struck pale with terror. Belgium was the first to respond to the cry of France, and she was free.

Liberal associations were reorganised on all sides and in every country, and strong endeavours were made to accelerate a universal movement. Germany, Italy and Spain were waiting but for the signal, and Poland, that ancient land of liberty, could not be left behind. It was in her very heart, too, that a revolution was to break forth; this was as necessary as unavoidable, for who had suffered more for independence, and who more ardently desired it? Placed between barbarism and civilization, her duty it was to elevate herself upon civilization, and exert a firm resistance against the barbarity which retained her captive.

She performed her duty, but unfortunately was not seconded. Little satisfied with the general conduct of the patriotic society, and impatient to shake off the ignominious yoke which bowed them down, several Poles, towards the month of October, formed two new secret societies, the one civil, the other military. The school of the ensign bearers was the focus of the last. There was congregated a set of young men, who were actually boiling over with enthusiasm and courage, but with that patriotism and courage which never reasons with duty, which knows not how to calculate the chances of success, and which never calculates, indeed, at all. Intrusted with these young hearts, these ardent and generous souls, the revolution does not linger on its way, but flies. Utopian plans and projects are laid aside; action is loudly called for; the cry is liberty or death.

In the meantime, the Russian Army begins to move, and the ambitious Nicholas orders it to chasten these French rebels, and stifle their new born liberty. The *Tzars* have set themselves up as apostles and champions of barbarity and absolutism. Wherever liberty raises its head, thither they order their herds of serfs to march. They have charge of the high police of all public places. Their interest requires that all should remain buried in the deepest ignorance, as well as the most brutish slavery. The disarming of the Polish troops was also seriously talked of, because they were suspected of entertaining some lurking desires for liberty; they were also suspected of plotting against the *Tzar* and his power.

The actual condition of the Poles was, indeed, a critical one. Must they renounce that future, which for so long a time, had been the subject of their dreams? Shall they basely bow their heads under the sword of the autocrat, and give passage to the armies which were going to fight against the sovereignty of the people, a people too who were their friends, their brothers? Or should they not rather rouse themselves, run to arms, break their chains, and proclaim the resurrection of Poland? The Pole never hesitates between glory and dishonour; and since, by his position, he found himself the van-guard of the camp of liberty, to him belonged the duty of encountering the first shock of the huge mass of iron which was advancing, with brutish and

59

savage barbarity, against the independence and civilization of nations. To him it belonged to break up, or, at least, arrest the destructive progress of this invading swarm; to him it belonged, even if he perished in the attempt.

The most alarming symptoms, for the Russian Government, were manifesting themselves all over the kingdom. The grand-duke now trembles, now threatens; the police is on the alert, spreads its nets, lets loose its spies and sends out its agents, succeeds even in catching hold of something like a clue to a conspiracy; they are on its track, reports are made, arrests ensue, and the convent of the Carmelites is crowded with prisoners. Not a moment is to be lost. Wysocki exclaims:

"The hour of vengeance has sounded, there is no longer time for delay—the die is cast—we must fight—to arms!"

At his voice the doors of the military school are broken open, and fall with a terrible crash. A handful of brave men rush thence into the city, calling the people to arms, and proclaiming independence ;—full of confidence in the justice of their noble cause, and their own courage, with a firm and steady step they go forward; they do not allow themselves to doubt of success; and yet they are about to face a powder which extends over more than one third of the earth's surface, and which may yet give laws to nearly all the nations of our globe.

A few minutes after this, Constantine w as seen flying from the city in which, for fifteen long years, he had exercised the functions of an executioner and corporal. Poland was free. Alas! it was but for a short time. Great God! has she not yet suffered enough for liberty? or has she been guilty of an offence so heinous, that thou canst not forgive her without wounding thine infinite justice! O! how long before the crown of her martyrdom may be awarded to her?

CHAPTER 8

Fears of the Russian Government

Notwithstanding the redoubled vigilance of the Russian police, and the fear of persecution, the news of the revolution of Warsaw soon spread, with astonishing rapidity, throughout all Lithuania. The blow, which it struck, was too strong not to resound simultaneously in every corner of Poland. It was like an electric discharge, which shakes instantaneously the whole chain, however long it may be. In less than three days, the news filled the space which separates the Vistula from the Dzwina, and inflamed every heart.

It was a spontaneous and sublime movement which pervaded every family of a great nation. Lithuania, above all, felt herself renovated—which, until that time, had dragged along her chains in hopeless indifference. But from this moment she was no longer the same; the blood circulated once more in a body which had been raised from the tomb. Like a man who hears in the distance, during the night, a mysterious voice, a hollow sound, she first raises her head a little, and looks intently in the direction whence the sound proceeds. She listens and starts to her feet; it is her sister, her mother, it is Poland, which calls her to arms and shows her how to break in sunder her chains.

But what can she do alone? Can she withstand the arms of the *Tzar*, who has his foot upon her breast? Can she repel far from her those battalions of Muscovite slaves, who retain her in slavery? She calls then upon the Poles, and, even with cries, implores their aid. Let them but come, let them appear, and Lithuania also will be free and unite herself to great Poland, never more to be separated from her. This great and sublime idea fills all hearts.

It is resolved to try everything, to do everything, in order to recover that liberty so precious, so beloved by every noble and great heart.—People are seen to run to and fro, they commune in secret whispers, they assemble in the depths of the woods, or in the solitary cottage; they talk to each other of newly conceived hopes, and of newly formed plans; they ply the forge, they prepare arms, they bring to light old swords, which have already, more than once, been employed upon the bodies of the Russians, in the time of the first wars for independence: they sharpen them anew, for the blows dealt by them must be mortal ones—he, who has been once struck by them, must never have the power of raising his arm against the liberty of Poland. Patriotism fires the hearts of all.

In the general enthusiasm, everyone is resolved to make great sacrifices. The noble and the rich resolve to sacrifice their property if necessary; the peasant and the workman, looking at their strong and muscular arms, calculate, in anticipation, the number of Russians which shall be prostrated by their individual valour. The events of the 29th of November are everywhere recounted, and with exaggerations; news is invented, which, as is usual in similar circumstances, greatly redounds to the honour of the favoured party, and which at least proves the spirit which reigns in Lithuania.

The Russian Government, astounded at the news of the sudden revolution, remained silent for some time, prosecuting, however, as disturbers of the public peace, whoever dared to mention it in public places. Perceiving, at last, that it was impossible to preserve the secret longer, it caused it to be publicly announced in the journal of Wilna, representing the whole affair however as an insignificant uproar of young men, whom His Majesty would soon chastise.

Measures are, at the same time, adopted for arresting the progress of the contagion, and keeping the Lithuanians to their duty. But what measures can a government, of such a character, take, which exists only for oppression, and which trembles with a consciousness of its own weakness? Shall it boldly face the public opinion which is opposed to it? Or shall it appeal to the affections of the people?

No, it is too cowardly to dare the first, and too well convinced of its own iniquity to place reliance upon the love of a people from which it merits nothing but hatred. Infamous itself, it can look for support to the infamous alone, and it is on the police that it places its chief reliance. This legion of spies, therefore, was reinforced by numerous recruits. These were of every sort; some were fops, handsome, delicately gloved and well perfumed, who were to insinuate themselves into the saloons of the first circles; others, the offspring of revolutions and constant enemies of good order, wherever existing, were to hang upon the steps of the students of Wilna, and take note of all their actions; and the task of such was no easy one, as they were obliged to render a daily account of themselves to Pelikan, with minute details of everything seen and heard. Others again were charged with the surveillance of citizens who were on the lists of the police. But soon the government, yielding to its fears, caused the suspected to be transported into the interior of Russia, and this by way of *precaution*. (Such was the expression of the *ukase* of the 24th of December, 1830).

The streets and coffee houses swarmed with secret agents declaiming against the government, in order to entrap the unwary, whom they would at once denounce, if caught in taking side with such sentiments.

Wherever four persons were accidentally met together, one of them was sure to be a spy; all confidence, between man and man, was destroyed. No one knew whom to trust, for even brother had been known to denounce brother and cause him to be thrown into a dungeon.

If on the one hand this plan of espionage afforded the government sure means of being informed of all that was going on, on the other it was far from being adapted to relieving it of its fears; for, in order to make themselves of greater importance, the secret agents would render most alarming reports, every moment, to the authorities, who were thereby kept in continual apprehension of danger, and hardly knew what to resolve upon.

Strong patrols were incessantly passing along the streets of the city, and whoever they met after nine o'clock, was a conspirator as a matter of course, and as such thrown into prison, unless he preferred the sacrifice of his purse, for in Russia everything can be bought—even liberty.

Lithuania was declared in a state of siege (a consequence quite natural to a country under a military government); but she was deprived of those small immunities generally granted in such cases, and which tend to soften the hardships of such a position.

The government ordered a levy of recruits, hut the peasants escaped to the woods to avoid this greatest of all calamities.

Under pretext of taking away, from the refractory, the means of resistance, the government ordered a general disarming of Lithuania, and caused to he seized arms of every description—guns, pistols, sabres, swords, daggers, hangers, and even the edged instruments of the kitchen, if their length rendered them, in the least, suspected. In vain did many citizens, having regard to the future, attempt to secure a few arms which were, in their estimation, the most highly prized of their personal effects. The blood-hounds of the police were sure to scent out these secret places of deposit, and the citizen guilty of such an act of rebellion, was but too fortunate if he could purchase, by means of gold, his life, threatened by the accusation of so terrible a crime against the state. They laid hands upon the implements of the chase, and the simple fusil even, used by the forester in driving off and destroying wild beasts, did not escape them.

Every day saw wagon loads of arms, the last hope of the patriots, deposited in the arsenal at Wilna; and yet not a word, not a sign, from Poland. She seemed to have forgotten her ancient limits, as well as those ancient brothers, beyond the Niemen, who were longing to fight with her, as well as for themselves.

After the first movement, the revolution, at Warsaw, took a decidedly wrong direction. The young men, who commenced it, were not ambitious, and never thought of aspiring to any dignity; and besides, they would not have exchanged their post of honour in front of the enemy, for the highest honour the state had to bestow. The government, therefore, remained in the hands of the authorities established by Nicholas, and everything was transacted in his name.

Sometime afterwards, the *doctrinaires* seized upon the reins of government;—these were men who, wedded to old customs, neither comprehended the intentions, nor understood the situation of the Poles. They contented themselves with protestations against the violation of the Charte, and demanded of Nicholas guaranties, when the nation was speaking of independence. For these, the Congress of Vienna had traced the limits of Poland, and their view extended not beyond. Indeed they would have declared the man a traitor, who would have dared to assert that partitions, made by violence and sustained by force, were null and void, and that it was necessary to extend the revolution into the invaded provinces.

It must be added also, that, judging the nation according to their imbecility, they believed it incapable of wrestling with Nicholas, whose faithful subjects they always acknowledged themselves to he, and to whom even they sent a deputation to make a regular report of the events which had taken place at Warsaw.

Clopicki took possession of the dictatorship; a skilful general and intrepid soldier, he might have rendered, and did, in fact, render, important services to the cause; but the camp is no place to acquire a knowledge of political manoeuvres, or the science of government. He shuddered at the danger which threatened Poland; he believed it on the brink of ruin, and saw no other chance of safety, but in the clemency of the *Tzar*. With his antiquated notions, he could never be persuaded that Poland could resist a power which had baffled Napoleon himself. Age having extinguished in him the intrepid bravery and fiery courage of youth, he submitted everything to the cold calculation of reason, and never took into account the prodigies of valour and the self-devotedness of a young and vigorous nation, and one which had determined to be free at whatever cost.

It is too often forgotten that men produced by a revolution, born, as it were, with it, are the only ones who can ensure its success. Great men of the past only obstruct its progress, they are incapable of imbibing its spirit.

The Polish revolution, in the hands of such men, soon came to a full stand. The grand-duke, instead of being retained as a hostage, was permitted freely to pass out of the kingdom, with those very troops, which returned to ravage it, three months after, and which might, at that time, easily have been disarmed. The men in power, listening neither to the counsel nor the wishes of the nation, contented themselves with merely acting upon the defensive, and tranquilly awaiting the enemy at the centre of the constitutional kingdom, instead of marching boldly forward to attack him at every vulnerable point.

In accordance with this deplorable system, Lithuania was placed entirely out of the question; and if, occasionally, certain Lithuanians, weary of the delay, and hurried on by their patriotism, would occasionally arrive at Warsaw and offer their services to the government, the dictator would reject their offer and their prayers, and would not look upon these over-zealous persons without vexation, who had come to disturb the pacific march which the skilful Lubecki had traced for the revolution, and which he, the dictator, had judged proper to adopt and to follow in every particular.

Whilst the Poles thus lost, by the indecision of its chief, all the advantage which it might have reaped from the panic spread among the Russians, these latter had time to recover their courage, and to concentrate their forces to crush the rebels. From all parts of the empire troops advanced by forced marches; the Siberian regiments traversed the immense space which separates them from Europe; the military colonies were put in motion; and towards the end of December all this mass spread over the plains of Lithuania, like an impetuous torrent, swollen by the snows of the Oural.

The corps of Pahlen, Schachoffskoi, Manderstren and Aurep, were pressing upon each other on their way to join themselves to the corps of Rosen, an ancient Lithuanian corps, which might have united itself to the Polish corps, if all the suspected officers had not been promptly removed from it and sent to Caucasia; this corps, afterwards, evinced the most violent animosity towards the Poles. It was with a bleeding heart that the Lithuanians saw such bodies of troops brought against Poland, which seemed abandoned to herself, and not able even to profit by her whole strength and the immense resources which Lithuania could have afforded her.

To look at these formidable masses, one would have thought that their number alone would suffice for effacing the slightest vestige of the small kingdom they were about to overrun. And yet, what terror depicted on their countenances! What pusillanimity in all their proceedings! The *prestige* attached to the name of Pole, the army of whose nation had always been proposed as a model to the Russian, had actually deprived them of their energy. Their march through Lithuania offered, already, the spectacle of an army disorganised by a fear which they endeavoured in vain to conceal. They advanced as if they had been in the midst of the enemy, in close order, with loaded muskets, and every precaution possible against ambuscades.

Every night, they expected the inhabitants would cut their throats; every forest appeared to them peopled with armed men, ready to fire upon them, and yet they could not have been ignorant of the fact, that the whole of Lithuania had been disarmed, and that, even if armed, she could not be able to struggle with their numerous columns.

At last, Diebitsch arrived at Wilna. The laurels gathered in Turkey could not conceal the fear which he shared with his army. He knew that he could not find in Poland *pachas* easy to be bribed. He knew the nation with which he was about to measure his strength, and he was inspired with a sad presentiment that the laurels of the Balkan would be in danger of fading on the foggy banks of the Vistula. Nevertheless, he affected arrogance and bravery, and proclaimed that he would merely have to pass over Poland to reach the south of Europe, and chastise those demagogues. But before leaving Wilna, the field marshal determined to secure the ground in the rear of his army, and establish the tranquillity of Lithuania.

Diebitsch, in a manner a soldier of fortune and destitute of country, could not comprehend the nature of such a thing as patriotism, and honestly believed that every revolution was the work of conspiracy. The focus of the revolt, both in Lithuania and elsewhere, was to be found, he thought, in the schools, and he determined to curry favour with the students of Wilna. He assembled them, therefore, and in a studied speech addressed to them, blamed the conduct of their superiors, regretted the vexations which the students had experienced from them, declared himself their protector, and promised gold and other favours, in reward for their fidelity. He finished by exhorting them to enter the army, promising instantly to exchange their academic grades for corresponding military ones.

★★★★★★

In Russia, the order of the different grades is strictly observed. Literary distinctions have also their classes, corresponding to civil and military grades. For instance, the first academic degree corresponds to the first grade of an army officer; a doctor's degree is equivalent to that of major in the army.

★★★★★★

This fine speech of the general was received in mournful silence; and a general cry of indignation drowned the voice of Pelikan, who next undertook to address them. These ardent youths, who dreamed of nothing but liberty and glory, were not seduced by such brilliant offers; not one of them entered the Russian Army, which so willingly opened its ranks to receive and load them with honours; but if they turned a deaf ear to the invitations of Diebitsch, they listened to their country's call summoning them to arms. What cared they for honours and wealth? All the reward they sought was to be in the foremost ranks of the army. More than two hundred of these heroic young men are now to be seen in France, more truly great in the plain *casaque* of the soldier, than many of our officers, so proud of their epaulettes and brilliant decorations obtained in the Russian or Austrian service.

Although the national government of Poland was slumbering, at the time it ought to have been engaged in energetic action, there were yet a few persons who had not forgotten Lithuania. At the head of these, was Lelewel, whose reputation for patriotism and knowledge, was as universal as it was well deserved. Being thoroughly acquainted with the character and spirit of the young men whom he had himself brought up, and by whom he was greatly beloved, he well knew the importance of their assistance; and in order to make up, as much as possible, for the deficiency of the men in power, sent James Grotkowski into Lithuania, with instructions to ascertain how the people stood affected towards the patriotic cause, to rouse and excite them to enthusiasm, and particularly the young, who, no doubt, would take the lead in any movements.

This young Lithuanian, who was at once brave, zealous, and intelligent, surmounted all the obstacles which this delicate mission afforded. (He was killed at the Battle of Haynowszczyzna, the 23rd of May, 1831). He eluded the argus-eyed police and penetrated as far as Wilna, when he became convinced that all the inhabitants of this ancient province of Poland were waiting, with impatience, the arrival of the Poles. Faithful to the instructions which he had received, he had an interview with those who had been particularly pointed out to him, made them acquainted with the particulars of the revolution at Warsaw, and instructed them in what they were to do, and in the expectations formed of them.

He did not conceal from them the dangers which threatened them, the fears which were entertained, and the limited resources of the republic; but he described, in glowing terms, the patriotism and enthusiasm which animated the entire population; and with that, everything might be hoped for. After having organised a committee of management, to whom he gave the watchword, he returned to Warsaw. Was this committee necessary, and was it useful? This may admit of a doubt. Committees are undoubtedly necessary in rousing from its lethargy a nation which is unmindful of its condition and insensible to the moral disease which is consuming it, and to prepare it for a revolution by gradually forming and directing public opinion.

But where this is already done, the people will revolutionise themselves, and require nothing but arms. Committees, in such case, serve only to embarrass the operations of the people, and are more injurious than useful. The men who compose these committees, seem to forget that an insurrection is a drama entirely made up of action, and which only needs direction, and not hindrance, and that everything must be made to concur in the unravelling of the plot which must be sudden, unavoidable, and unforeseen, else everything is jeoparded. Success is alone to be expected from patriotism, courage and good fortune, not from arguments and indecision.

They waste their time in the debates of the assembly, they weigh their *pros* and *cons*, prepare their plans, engage in intrigues, consume precious time in preparations, and, in the meantime, enthusiasm is quenched, the enemy, taken at first by surprise, recovers his courage, ascertains the number of his assailants, rallies his forces, and all is lost.

We have a striking proof of this in Lithuania. The people, impatient of the yoke imposed upon them, wished to revolt with their whole force, and were rendered indignant at being held in check; whilst the blunders of the Russian government placed, as it were, their army in the power of the Lithuanians. Placing too great reliance upon the disarming of the country, Diebitsch conceived the project of drawing from Lithuania, all the necessary supplies for the Polish war. The Russian Army entered the kingdom destitute of provisions, relying upon Lithuania for necessary supplies.

Immense stores were ordered, with directions to transport them to the frontiers of Poland. This was the easiest, and the most direct method. The military purveyors were put to very little trouble in procuring supplies, and the treasure was not drawn upon. A sheet of paper converted into an *ukase*, was all that was needed. But, at the same time, this manner of proceeding placed the Russian government completely at the mercy of the Lithuanians, who, not having the means of assisting their compatriots by means of arms, could send famine into the camp of their enemies.

Notwithstanding this advantage, and the imperious voice of duty, the committee dared not to decide. They were waiting, and so were the people, but in a violent rage at the restraints imposed upon them. The time for raising the levy of recruits was near at hand, the furnishing of provisions had commenced, and the roar of cannon was already heard in the direction of Warsaw. Every true patriot felt that every moment was precious, and tired, at length, at the delay of the committee, resolved to act.

Julius Gruzewski, one of the most ardent, judged the moment favourable; and alarmed, perhaps, at the news of the arrest of Staniewicz, at Libau, assembled a small troop of thirty men, and placing himself at their head, on the 25th of March, 1831, drove the Russians from the city of Rossien. The whole country responded to this signal, and Lithuania, destitute of arms, threw down the gauntlet to Russia. From this time the committee was a perfect nullity. The sword alone was to decide the contest. Sublime and terrible moment, when the weaker rise against the stronger, and endeavour to overthrow them! a moment in which a handful of brave men, without arms, without leaders, animated by the love of country and of liberty, sustained by their own courage, and armed by hatred against tyranny, raise the cry of independence, and rush upon an enemy a thousand times more numerous than themselves, and which they cause to tremble.

Such instances of patriotism and deep devotedness are rare in the annals of nations.

CHAPTER 9

Her First Victory

Emily Plater could not rest tranquil, when all about her was animated with a new life. The revolution of the 29th of November did not come upon her unprepared. The cry of liberty, rising from the banks of the Vistula, had reached her ears, and it met with a deep response from her own heart. She saw the dreams of her whole youth about to be realised. She could now sacrifice herself upon the altar of her country's good; she could now labour, even she, a weak woman, in rescuing her country from slavery. How this idea made her leap for joy! She felt herself inspired with a new life.

Proud and intrepid, she rose a cubit in stature. She would have challenged any warrior, or hero, to compete with her in courage or intrepidity. She would have seized the helmet and sword, mounted horse, and rushed with boldness into the very midst of the Muscovite battalions, whom she hated, and whom she would have trodden under foot and a thousand times destroyed, had they possessed but one head, even if she had perished herself in the act. To die for her country seemed to her one of the noblest of actions.

Like all the Lithuanians, Emily had been expecting the arrival of the Poles, and she thought she would have nothing else to do but to serve her country, mingled with the crowd of warriors. But the errors of the government, at Warsaw, soon destroyed her hopes, and opened for her courage a career much more extensive, and imposed upon her a task of greater difficulty, but one which afforded greater scope for great and noble deeds. Emily said:

The country, is not responsible for the folly of the men in power.

And, far from being disheartened at the apathy and indifference exhibited by this government towards their compatriots, she laboured constantly to sustain the enthusiasm in weak and undecided minds, which, carried away by the torrent, are willing, at the first moment, to make any sacrifice, but which, as soon as the first impulse has subsided, are too ready to fall back into the apathy and torpor natural to them.

Where the government of a country is so constituted that its principal strength consists solely in the nobility, and where the people are plunged into the darkness of ignorance and servitude, (and such unhappily is the condition of all the countries of the north,) in such a country, the influence of a single individual is capable of powerful action upon the masses, and of imparting to them an impulse; particularly if by her position in society, her talents and her genius, she can command their respect, while, by her acts of kindness, she can attract to herself their love and confidence.

Emily, always gentle and compassionate, was beloved and respected in the neighbouring parts, as much by the peasants as by the nobility. She made no other use of the influence which her birth, her virtues and her education afforded her, but to employ it in aid of the holy cause of her country. She was persuaded that the people ardently loved their country and hated the Russians, but that they were not sufficiently enlightened to guide themselves.

Maintaining constant intercourse with them, she profited, by her position, in giving them some direction. She explained to them the causes of delay, on the part of their Polish brethren, gave them reason to hope that the obstacles would soon be surmounted, that in a few days they would have it in their power to unite with their brothers in Poland, in ridding themselves of the Russian yoke, and she counselled them that, while awaiting this event, they should hold themselves prepared for every occasion, and should conceal, with great care, the arms of which the Russians wished to despoil them.

The people listened to her counsels and followed them, because they saw her constantly occupied in promoting the welfare of the country.

After having disposed their minds in favour of the cause of liberty, and fully convinced herself that the whole neighbourhood would rise and march at the first signal, Emily set out for Wilna, in order to concert measures with the directing committee, and to take instructions for her future conduct. But she forgot that she was a woman, and that men affect an exclusive monopoly in politics, courage and wisdom. Her sex excluded her from that confidence which her enterprising character, and extensive designs, ought to have secured to her, rather than to two-thirds of the members which composed the committee, and her journey was unsuccessful.

Thus, left alone in her career and patriotic intentions, by the ignorant presumption of the men, Emily, nevertheless, ceased not to occupy herself with her favourite scheme, and conceived an enterprise as great and as bold as her own heart. She wished to show to the men that she, also, was capable of great things.

The fortress of Dünabourg, situated upon the other side of the Dzwina, was not far distant from her own residence. To take possession of this half-fortified city, and of the immense arsenal there; to hoist, upon the left bank of the Dzwina, the standard of the white eagle, and of the Lithuanian order of knights; to call the inhabitants to arms; to awaken, in their hearts, the weak, but not yet extinguished recollections of their former relations with the Poles, and thus transfer the insurrection into Livonia and western Russia,—such were the projects conceived by Emily Plater, and which she wished to execute. Having lived from infancy in the neighbourhood of this city, she well knew the weakness of the garrison, and the disorder which generally reigns in a place in which a large number of workmen are assembled, and the commander of which, full of security, was in little expectation of being attacked on his post, in the midst of such a peaceable population.

The young heroine was perfectly well acquainted with all the weak points of the place, at which it could be easily entered. She even procured a plan of the city, with its fortifications, and after having carefully considered the chances, she decided on an attempt to surprise it.

Is it not surprising to see a young girl, weak and inexperienced, conceive, and put in execution, a project of this kind, and that, too, with deliberation, with the exercise of the greatest caution and prudence, and without forgetting anything that could, in the least, influence its success? She must, indeed, have possessed a genius eminently military, a soul full of ardour, touched with the most lofty patriotism, and one which sported with danger.

To ensure success, she endeavoured to effect a communication with the interior of the fortress.

In Russia, by statute law, it is rendered obligatory, on the part of the nobility, to obtain, by actual service, a grade in the military or civil service, before being entitled to the rights of citizenship. The disgrace attached to a civil office, on account of the venality and corruption of the government, induces everyone to prefer the army. The Lithuanians, not being able to enter into the Polish Army, saw themselves obliged to enrol themselves in the ranks of the Russian Army, in order to meet the requisitions of the law; and they composed the chief part of the military school established at Dünabourg, for the subalterns of the army.

Polish hearts were beating under the Russian uniform, which they were obliged to wear, and thoughts of liberty would produce a thrill of delight in the bosoms of these youths, who were as patriotic as they were eager for fame. Among them were two cousins of Emily's. She laid open to these her mind and her plans, and found that they, too. had formed the same design. They, too, felt the importance of the place in effecting the Polish revolution, as well as that which was in a state of preparation in Poland.

They were long in concerting their plan, and it was finally agreed that, on the approach of Emily and the insurgents, the military school should rise, take arms, fall unexpectedly upon the garrison of the citadel, and thus essentially contribute to the taking of the place.

There was but one thing further, which retarded Emily, and this was the committee. Persuaded, like everyone else, that this committee was acting in accordance with instructions from Warsaw, and that it was incumbent upon them to give the signal for revolt, she feared, by too great precipitation, to injure the cause by arousing the suspicions of the oppressors. This fear was still exerting an influence upon her when Gruzewski, as we have already mentioned, struck the first blow and gave the signal.

Without loss of time, Emily went to work; she rouses the conspirators to action, and entreats them to follow her. She desires to be among the first to proclaim that the reign of Russia is ended. She possesses as much patriotism as anyone else, and longs to partake of the common danger. On the 29th of March, she parts with her golden tresses, assumes man's attire, arms herself with pistols and a dirk; and followed by Mademoiselle Pruszynska and two young men, she repairs to the village of Dousiaty, where everything was in a state of readiness. They were only awaiting the arrival of Caesar Plater, (the proprietor of the village, and who happened at that time to be absent at Wilna,) before unfolding the sacred banner of revolt, which, in the present case, was also that of justice. This young patriot, who will occupy such a prominent place in the sequel of this history, saw, not without pain, the slow progress of affairs; he was incessantly going backwards and forwards, and endeavouring with all his might to accelerate the time for acting.

It was Sunday. A much greater number of people had collected from the neighbourhood, to throng the church, than usual; attracted by mysterious rumours of something new being in agitation. At the sight of the young countess in arms and mounted, the multitude began to crowd to the public square, where the national standard had already been unfurled by the hands of our heroine. In a brief and animated speech, she explained the powerful motives which were calling the country to arms.

It is not by vain and idle words that she endeavours to rouse them and engage them to join her. It is in the name of their own interest that she addresses them. She dwells upon the extortions to which they are subjected by the Russians, the burdensome taxes which weigh them down, the army conscriptions which wrest their children from them, and whom they can never see more, the persecutions of the police, etc. She cries to them:

> It is time, it is time to go and aid our Polish brothers, who are fighting for us upon the shores of the Vistula. We must break the chains which overwhelm us, we must be free, we must fight; God wills it!!!

No one can resist this powerful appeal of a new crusade against barbarity and oppression. No heart is closed against the cry of liberty. These words sink down into the very depths of the soul, they overcome every obstacle, they gain the complete mastery of every heart. The multitude respond to Emily with shouts of enthusiasm, admiration and hatred. They hold in abhorrence, and trample underfoot, the monster whose hand has so long kept ancient Poland in a state of intolerable oppression. They wish to be free, and they will be so. The hatred which has always lived in the depths of their hearts, once more awakes, powerful and terrible. It is face to face, hand to hand, that they will say to the Russians that they are hated, and that they are wanted no longer.

The young men run, armed with scythes and pikes, among which are occasionally seen to glisten a few fowling-pieces. In less than a quarter of an hour the village assumes a warlike attitude. Cartridges are distributed, and the insurgents are organised. The blacksmith is busy in converting the scythes into warlike instruments, which hereafter are to be employed in breaking in sunder the chains of their oppressors. The whole day is spent in preparations, amidst noise and confusion. Emily Plater superintends everything; nothing escapes her oversight and unwearied activity. She is the soul of the insurrection.

Every moment, fresh bodies of volunteers are coming in from every direction to place themselves under the command of a *woman*, but a woman who has already given proof of her great energy, whom they know, whom they all esteem and almost worship.

The next day, she seized the horses of the Dangiele post-office, amounting to about thirty, and with this addition to her cavalry, she began her march on Dünabourg, at the head of two hundred and eighty *chasseurs*, several hundred *faucheurs*, and a body of *caviliers* amounting to sixty. (*Chasseurs* are light cavalry; *faucheurs*, men armed with scythes; *caviliers*, mounted gentlemen). She presses the march in order to take the city by surprise. But the country through which the march lies is still tranquil, and the population must be roused, armed and organised, and, above all, made to feel the necessity of prompt and vigorous action. All this retards every moment her march, and embarrasses her plans, the success of which depends almost entirely upon celerity. Moreover, a company of Russian infantry are on the way, from Ucinia to Dünabourg, to intercept her march. Emily attacks them on the 2nd of April, and, after an obstinate contest, forces the enemy to yield.

After a painful march of several days, she arrived, at last, at Jeziorossy. But the alarm had already been given to the commander at Dünabourg, who sent two companies of infantry to arrest the insurgents. The Russians, trusting to their strength and number, advanced with confident expectation of dispersing these rebels, who were marching without order or munitions.

Emily was advised of the approach of the enemy and did not seek to avoid them; she rather desired to meet them, in order to exercise her troop and impart confidence to her own forces; she knew what might be effected by means of enthusiasm and resolution. She was persuaded that a victory, however slight it might be, would open the way to a thousand victories besides. She wished, by an unexpected and bold attack, to infuse terror into the Russians; she did not, therefore, hesitate to attack them as soon as she met them.

It was near the village of Jeziorossy, on the 4th of April, at break of day, that she fell upon their camp, routed them, threw them into utter confusion, and finished by achieving a complete victory. The Russians had no expectation of this attack. They believed the enemy to be struck with fear, and incapable of undertaking anything. Seeing themselves vigorously pressed by an enemy which they had despised, they supposed that he had received reinforcements; they did not, therefore, defend themselves with vigour, but soon gave way, leaving about sixty of their own, killed or wounded. Emily, proud of this victory, pushed on, took possession of the village of Jeziorossy and pursued the fugitives on the high road to Dünabourg, where she expected to arrive as soon as they, and risk the action which was, perhaps, to decide the campaign.

CHAPTER 10

Emily joins the corps of Charles Zaluski

If courage and contempt of death had been alone sufficient to make an enterprise succeed, Emily Plater would doubtless have carried all her plans triumphantly through. But a chief has need of something else, besides excellent qualities. He needs arms and soldiers. How can he, with a small troop, badly armed and without munitions, maintain his position in presence of an enemy twenty times more numerous, and abounding in resources?

The small army of Emily, which had, at the beginning of the campaign, but a very small number of cartridges, had almost completely consumed them in the two first engagements. She nevertheless advanced; but she could rely on none but the *faucheurs*; the lack of powder and ball rendering their muskets useless. And what a weapon, the scythe! It is suitable for holding the third rank in the line, excellent in the pursuit of an enemy already routed by regular troops, but very seldom have the *faucheurs* been known to break close columns and decide the battle.

Thus, it was impossible for our friends to resist successfully the regular troops, and the commander at Dünabourg, advised by the fugitives of the fate of his first detachment, sent a battalion of infantry, with two pieces of cannon, against the enemy who were advancing, and at the same time, *raising the country*. The affair could not be doubtful; after a short contest the insurgents, broken at all points, dispersed. Fighting without any order, they were not able to rally; and closely pressed by the Russians, who pursued them for a long distance, Emily was obliged to retrace her steps, and had the grief to see all the villages which she had delivered retaken by the enemy, who exercised upon them the greatest cruelties. Dousiaty, where the standard of insurrection had been for the first time unfolded by her own hand, was taken by the Russians, and consigned to the flames.

Moreover, the plan of Emily, for surprising Dünabourg, had become impracticable by a number of changes which had been made in that fortress. The young men on whom Emily had most relied, had all been sent away. Whether the Russian general entertained any suspicion of the plot, or whether, alarmed by the progress of the insurrection, he feared to retain in the fortress men whose fidelity was, to say the least, very doubtful, and whom national affinity with the rebels would lead to sympathize with them, he caused them to be disarmed and sent off, on the 9th of April, to the army of Diebitsch, under escort of a detachment of the imperial guard.

★★★★★★

These young men, eighteen in number, succeeded in making their escape from their guard during the journey, and were afterwards of great service to the Polish cause.

★★★★★★

This decision of the Russian commander, and the check which she had just experienced, destroyed all the plans of Emily. After having collected the shattered remains of her little troop, she united them to the command of her cousin, Count Caesar Plater, quitted the neighbourhood of Dousiaty, and, followed only by Mademoiselle Pruszynska, went to join the corps of insurgents under the command of Zaluski.

Some days after the revolution had broken out in Lithuania, the insurgents, seeing that all their operations were conducted without order and without any favourable result, each corps acting separately, resolved to appoint a commander in chief, who should unite all the different corps, and by this means be able to strike a decisive blow. It was difficult to find a man capable of this trust, and at the same time worthy of their confidence. The Lithuanians having, for twenty years, crouched under the yoke of Russia, had devoted themselves exclusively to private life and to agriculture. No one among them had devoted himself to the military service, and if any veteran of the legions was still to be found in the ranks of the insurgents, most frequently he lacked a name which could inspire the people with confidence and command their respect.

Count Charles Zaluski, leader of the insurrection in the district of Upita, was distinguished by an unexampled activity and zeal. The choice fell upon him, and he was proclaimed commander in chief by the insurgents of Wilna, Wilkomierz, Troki, Kowno, Oszmiana and Upita. Although a zealous patriot, governed by the purest motives, and of undaunted bravery, yet, being but a mere novice in the art of war, he was unwilling to accept a charge involving so much responsibility. It was, nevertheless, insisted upon, and he could not refuse.

The secret committee of Wilna were constantly sending emissaries to urge Zaluski to unite all the forces, and come with them to attack Wilna, promising him the rising of the whole town, and a complete success in expelling the Russians from Lithuania. Zaluski well knew the futility of this project, and was perfectly assured that it would be impossible for him to take possession of a city fortified on all sides, bristling with cannon, and long prepared for any attack whatever. But still pressed by the committee and the other insurgents, obeying, moreover, the impulse of his own heart, with a strong desire to free his country in the shortest time possible, he set out......Braving danger, in every engagement he added much to his reputation; but, at the distance of five leagues from the capital, he was vanquished by the Russians, in consequence of the inexperience of the insurgents, and constrained to retreat, and, finally, to retire to the neighbourhood of Wilna.

When Emily Plater joined him, he was encamped near Smilgi, in the district of Upita. Her renown had preceded her, and everyone was curious to become acquainted with the woman, who not only had given an example to the men, but who had even surpassed them by her devotedness, the boldness of her plans, and her promptness in the execution of them. They ran in crowds to see and admire her; but, with the most part, this admiration was cold and constrained.

Romantic young men hoped to find in her an amazon of brilliant *parure*, a female warrior like those seen at the theatre; but how great was their disappointment at the sight of a woman dressed in a plain blue *casaque* of coarse cloth, and entirely destitute of that brilliant exterior which is so imposing to the vulgar, and which is often mistaken for real merit! Others, again, regarding with a jealous eye a woman who had dared to invade the rights of the male sex, and, influenced by a pitiful jealousy which could not forgive her the glory with which she had covered herself, gave her a cold reception, and under pretence of zeal and solicitude for a life so precious, would endeavour to divert her from her martial schemes.

They said to her:

You are a woman, Countess, and you can never endure the fatigues of the camp. We are far from questioning your courage and talents; but battles and the prospect of death, which constantly threaten us, are the least of our troubles. You, whose complexion is so delicate, would you be able to pass your nights without sleep, your days without rest, and sometimes without food?

Would you be able to perform forced marches, of fifteen leagues, through dense forests destitute of roads, or impracticable marshes'? Could you swim over rivers? No, Countess, your health would sink under such fatigues. Resume, then, your female pursuits, and be satisfied with the glory and gratitude, which are so justly your due, and preserve that health which, for many reasons, is so dear to us. But if you wish to be useful to your country, are there not other ways of serving her, besides bearing arms? A grand and noble career is now opened to your sex, which is unquestionably more congenial to your taste. Bestow all your cares upon the wounded.

Emily would listen coldly to such remarks, and would sometimes answer:

I know that my health and arm are both weak; but the arms I wear are merely for my own defence. These pistols will protect me from personal danger, when attacked by an enemy, and if these fail me, this dirk, which you see, will not allow me to be taken alive.

But, gentlemen, (added she with a faint smile), I am a woman, and, as such, cannot overcome the curiosity which impels me to assist in your battles, and be an eye-witness of your courage; and, finally, to dress your noble wounds on the spot, and at the moment you receive them. As to these fatigues, weak as I am, I know how to endure them.

These officious advisers, rebuked by this polite, though slightly ironical answer, held their peace, and durst not oppose her views any further.

On the next day. May the 4th, Zaluski marched to Przystowiany, at which place the commander in chief, incorrectly informed with respect to the position of the enemy, as he supposed him to be far distant, proposed to grant a few days' repose to his troops, fatigued, as they were, by three weeks' marching and counter-marching. They arrived at Przystowiany at about eleven o'clock in the morning. Emily Plater immediately repaired to the encampment of the free *chasseurs* of Wilkomir, and requested that they would admit her into their ranks. This corps, who were for the most part composed of the principal citizens of the country, and who had already given many signal proofs of their devotedness and valour, proud of the choice Emily had made, received her among them with acclamation. They considered such a recruit an honour to their corps, and its commander determined to celebrate the event by a kind of military *fête*.

But while preparations for this fete were making, and the rest of the insurgents were resting, in all security, after the fatigues of their long march, a discharge of musketry upon their left wing, which was partly composed of the students of Wilna, gave notice, at about one o'clock, p. m., of the approach of the enemy.

Soon the Russian lancers were seen deploying on the plain, and the infantry marching in close column. This force was composed of two regiments of cavalry, one brigade of infantry, and twelve pieces of cannon, all under command of Generals Sulima and Malinowski; they were marching against us.

The insurgents, taken by surprise, seized their arms, and hastened to take position in a small wood which crowned the summit of a hill.

"These Russian gentlemen are very impolite to come to molest our *fête* in this manner," observed the commander of the free *chasseurs*, with a smile, and who had already stood fire in the service of the French, under Napoleon.

"They come to grace it," cried Emily, seizing her musket; "they will give me opportunity of proving to you that I am worthy of being your companion in arms."

In an instant, everyone was at his post; the fire of the Russians was brisk, and the cannon roared.

The Russian infantry advanced to dislodge, at the point of the bayonet, the insurgents from their cover; these allowed them to advance within fifty paces. Fire! cries the commander of the *chasseurs*. A simultaneous discharge of musketry ensues, and the Russians are thrown into confusion by the murderous volley, and are this time repulsed with great loss.

A second attempt of the enemy in like manner failed, and the insurgents by no means despaired of maintaining their position, which had been already contested for four hours.

How painful to be forced to relinquish the victory to the enemy, in a moment when it seems to be within your grasp! How unfortunate that resources should not correspond with courage and justice! But such is the fate of battles.

"Cartridges! We want cartridges," suddenly and almost simultaneously cried all the *chasseurs*.

"We have no more," sorrowfully replied the commander. All at once the whole line of insurgents rung with a shriek of despair, for they must yield.

Regular troops, however well disciplined, rarely retreat with order; how then could it be otherwise with the insurgents, who were entirely ignorant of discipline? As long as they had ammunition, they stood their ground, but once obliged to yield, they dispersed in the greatest disorder. It was not so much a retreat as a complete helter-skelter. The confusion was, if possible, increased by the giving way of a defective bridge thrown over a small river, which they were obliged to wade, with water up to the chin. All the muskets, which remained charged, were of course wet in this passage, and all further resistance was out of question. The Russians pursued, for a long time, cutting down all whom they overtook.

This day would have been entirely fatal to the insurgents, had not Maurice Prozor heard, by good fortune, the firing, and hastened, with his command, to cover their retreat, by directing a murderous fire upon the enemy's cavalry.

During the battle, Emily was in the front line, passing from rank to rank, braving death, without however inflicting it. At the commencement of the retreat, she found herself in a critical position. Deserted by her own people, in the midst of the general confusion, with only three men near her, she was slowly retiring, when the Russians, already in possession of the main road, endeavoured to cut off her retreat, and several advanced to lay hold on her. A dozen guns were fired close to her, which Emily did not think proper to return, and prevented her companions from firing, she cried:

"Save your powder, temerity is useless and imprudent. What could we four do against that cloud of Russians, which is pursuing us? Instead then of wasting our time on the road, let us endeavour to gain ground on them. If we are cut off from every means of retreat, then indeed will we sell our lives as dearly as we can, and prevent ourselves from being taken alive."

The ground they were obliged to go over had been lately ploughed, and the recent rains had made it so soft as to greatly retard the progress of the cavalry, while it afforded considerable advantage to those on foot. However, Emily, much fatigued by the battle and her flight, made but slow progress. Continually exposed to the enemy's fire, and almost within hearing of the breathing of their horses, she nevertheless gained ground on those in pursuit, and succeeded at length in reaching a forest, when she fell, overcome with fatigue.

Nothing on earth would have induced the Russians to enter a wood, which their imagination always represented to them as swarming with insurgents, placed in ambuscade; the pursuit, therefore, here ended. Towards evening, Emily crawled to the cottage of a forester, not more than five hundred yards from the Russian camp, whence the sentry's call was plainly heard. But she was so much exhausted that she was obliged to stay all night in this insecure place, exposed every moment to being captured by the enemy.

The next day, feeling a little recovered, she resumed her retreat. The country was covered with Russians, and crossed and recrossed in every direction by their detachments. Although entirely ignorant of the place the troops of Zaluski had retired to, yet she succeeded in rejoining them on the banks of the Doubissa, leading with her a detachment of forty men, which she had rallied during her painful and dangerous retreat.

CHAPTER 11

Mary Raszanowicz and Emily Plater

After the unfortunate affair at Przystowiany, the chiefs of the insurrection, perceiving that the uniting of several detachments into one corps, so far from being useful to the cause, served, but to leave the country unprotected and exposed to the resentments of the Russians, determined to divide the troops into small parties, and to return home. This arrangement would, at least, afford them an opportunity of exerting their personal influence and of profiting by their knowledge of localities; whilst, united, they could do little else than march from one place to another, without any object or result.

In consequence of this decision, Charles Zaluski and Leon Potocki returned into the district of Upita; Vincent Matuszewicz took to the forests of Troki with his insurgents, thence to spread terror into the Russian ranks. The free *chasseurs* of Wilcomir, to which Emily Plater belonged, took up the march for their own district.

Their arrival was opportune; for already the fruits of their first success were lost. Werzulin, with his *Circassians*, (the same Werzulin whose cruelty recalled the memory of Souvaroff and Drevitsch,) was master of Wilkomir. The police, under protection of the troops, had resumed their usual course; the spies were active, the Jews were denouncing peaceable citizens and persecutions again commenced with renewed violence. The desire of liberating their friends, their brothers, not less than that of avenging, upon Werzulin, the blood of the women and children massacred at Oszmiana, impelled the free *chasseurs* to advance on Wilkomir, and after a consultation, on the part of Col. Charles Przezdziecki, Plater, Grolkowski and the chiefs of the insurrection of Wilna, they laid siege to the place on the 17th of May, before sunrise.

But Werzulin, brave in the massacre of women, and a coward in battle, seeing the insurgents advancing on all sides, thought it more prudent to abandon the city, marking his retreat by murder, rape and fire.

The insurgents, once more masters of the chief place of the district, sent several detachments in pursuit of this brigand, and applied themselves to the organisation of the country. They established a provisionary government, which was charged with the administration of public affairs, the maintaining of internal tranquillity and the providing for the immediate wants of the insurrection. It was during these transactions that a young insurgent presented himself to the chief of the troops, and offered his services. His delicate features, slender form, and fine curls, belied his dress. It was no other than young Mary Raszanowicz, who also wished to try her fate in war. A blooming beauty of twenty, she naturally possessed the happy faculty of supporting reverses with gayety, without, however, exposing herself to the charge of indifference.

Long and fatiguing marches, the hardships of the camp, the soldier's coarse fare, could none of them make any impression on her gay and cheerful temper. She could be playful in the midst of danger, and laugh in the presence of death. Her mirth was without affectation or malice. She was plain, gentle, frank and engaging in her manners; but subsequently, the misfortunes of her country, which greatly afflicted her, imparted a tinge of sadness to her character. But at the time of which we are speaking, nothing, as yet, portended ill to Poland, which, everywhere victorious, was almost sure of regaining her ancient independence.

The identity of sex and feeling soon united her to Emily in the bonds of the most intimate friendship; their warm, enthusiastic young hearts understood each other at once. Both wished to toil and fight in the cause of their country. From that day, they were inseparable; they solemnly pledged themselves to fight, side by side, like two brothers in arms, and to share the same fortune, whether good or bad. They kept their faith. Death alone has separated them; Mary Raszanowicz has received the last breath of Emily Plater.

Those officious advisers, who, once before, had been so well rebuked, returned to the charge, and again attempted to dissuade Emily from what they chose to term her mania for war. The recent danger, which she had encountered at Przystowiany, served them as a pretext for obtruding their officious advice upon her, and to constrain her to retire to the protection of one of her relatives, who lived in the neighbourhood of Wilkomir.

Emily Plater, weary of these babblers, and wishing to avoid the annoyance, resolved to join another corps.

Parczewski was then intending to advance on Wilna, and reassume the positions in which he had maintained himself for the two successive months, affording, the meanwhile, the most signal proofs of courage and coolness, keeping the enemy constantly on the alert, harassing them, and attacking them when he had the least prospect of success. Although, in approaching Wilna, he would be more exposed to the attacks of the Russians, yet it would place it in his power to communicate with the patriots of Wilna, and concert measures with them; he would also be within reach of a thousand resources which that great city could afford. He was about to place himself, as it were, upon the van of the troops, and this position would offer him more opportunities for attacking the enemy, and also more dangers to encounter. These considerations determined Emily Plater to select this corps. She therefore, with her new and inseparable friend, Mary Raszanowicz, went to join that corps.

Six leagues from Wilna, Parczewski, misinformed in regard to the enemy's movements, fell into an ambuscade, and it was after considerable loss, that he finally succeeded in extricating himself from his perilous situation. He went to encamp at Olany, where the Russians did not dare to molest him; he passed eight days quietly in this camp, recruiting his men and procuring ammunition, of which the several engagements that he had encountered had nearly exhausted him, and which could with difficulty be procured, at a high price, and at the risk of life.

In other respects, the last week of May and the first part of June passed without any remarkable events. There was, on both sides, a kind of armistice brought on by circumstances. They apparently seemed to be resting from the toils of war. The Russians were compelled to allow their army some rest, fatigued and harassed by a sort of partisan war of two months, during which they had been obliged, every day, to act on the offensive or defensive, without obtaining any decided advantage, or being able to force the insurgents to a decisive engagement. They therefore ceased to chase the rebels, and waited for General Tolstoi, whom the emperor had appointed commander-in-chief of the army of reserve, and who was coming from Western Russia, with a considerable force, in order to crush the insurgents by their number, and put an end, at once, to the rebellion.

The insurgents, who had been several times dispersed by the Russians, had also need of repose, in order to rally anew, and did not think of attacking the enemy. The news of the march of Tolstoi alarmed them the more, as already, without reinforcement, the enemy was four times their own number, and they, moreover, lacked powder and shot. After an inspection of their ammunition, the chiefs were convinced that, even if their detachments were reduced one third, each soldier would hardly be supplied with more than five rounds apiece; the messengers they had despatched in every direction to procure a supply, would return with but a small quantity, and often with none.

From the other side of the Niemen, nothing could be heard, and there was no news from Poland, which indeed seemed to have forgotten us, and entirely left us to our own resources to contend single-handed with the Russian Army, which allowed us no repose. The moment of decision had come. The most prevailing opinion was in favour of disbanding the troops, and of the bravest, together with those most deeply committed in the insurrection, reassembling, and, in close columns, forcing a passage through the Russian battalions, in order to join the Polish Army. Some, however, were far from favouring this opinion. Resolved to shed the last drop of blood, they wished to remain in the country, maintain the insurrection, and keep the Russian troops at bay until the arrival of the Poles, who could not much longer delay to march to the assistance of their brethren.

It may well be imagined that Emily Plater was of this last opinion, and that she never could entertain for a moment the idea of abandoning Lithuania to the Russians, she said:

The Lithuanians, weak as they are, keep busy twenty thousand Russians, who otherwise would go to reinforce Diebitsch's army. Besides, as long as the insurrection lasts, the enemy can reap no advantage from the resources of the country; his communication with St. Petersburg is cut off, or, at least greatly impeded. In abandoning the country, we voluntarily resign to the enemy all these advantages, and what have we to offer to the Poles in return? The insignificant assistance of a few hundred men. Death can overtake us as easily there as here; it might perhaps be more glorious in Poland, but here it will, at least, be more useful to the common cause. Let us perish, if necessary, but let us perish with honour; and let us not forsake those we ourselves have excited to insurrection; they have intrusted us with their defence, and we have sworn to free them from oppression.

CHAPTER 12

Battle of Kowno

While the chiefs of the insurrection were in a state of indecision, Constantine Zaleski arrived in the midst of them, with orders from Gen. Chlapowski to the insurgents, that they should immediately take up the line of march to join the Polish troops, which were advancing towards Lida.

This unexpected news inspired the insurgents, as well as the inhabitants, with new hopes and new courage, although ignorant of the amount of force with Chlapowski. They entertained no doubt but that, with the help of the Poles, they could not only successfully oppose the Russians, but even triumph over them. Men skilled in the military art would know how to organise and drill these masses of insurgents, who, thus far, had been able merely to revolutionize the country, and keep the enemy in a state of constant alarm, but not entirely to subdue him; the insurgents, too, had to this time been destitute of a chief.—We were satisfied that even the sight of the Poles would revive the enthusiasm of our citizens, as well as the courage of the army, which a series of disasters had begun to repress.

Chlapowski, it was said, was bringing with him artillery as well as small arms, which he had taken from the enemy, in forcing his passage through the Russian Army, over which he had even obtained some advantage. We had no further doubts as to the future; victory, now, seemed to us certain. We looked upon Chlapowski as a saviour, and no one dreamed any longer of abandoning Lithuania. The general voice was:

"Let us not hesitate, every moment is precious, let us go and join our brethren, let us prove, by our readiness to obey orders, that we are worthy of freedom."

But as the Lithuanians had, for some time past, relinquished the hope of receiving assistance from Poland, many of them looked upon this unexpected news, of the actual approach of the Poles, as improbable; and it raised doubts in the minds of men, whose circumspection amounts to distrust, and who are inclined to give the worst construction to every event, they would say:

"We have so often been deceived on this point, that we may yet well doubt it. And what evidence can this man, who has come to announce to us the approach of our friends, afford us of the truth of his assertion? Might he not be a spy sent by the enemy to induce us to leave our position, and betray us and the country to the rage and vengeance of the Russians? Let us act with prudence, and, in the first place, send a confidential messenger to ascertain the truth of this information; then, on his return, we can act with perfect safety."

Such thoughts, secretly disseminated among the insurgents, shook their belief, and soon many detachments declared that they would not leave their position, without some convincing proofs.

Poor Zaleski was at a loss to know how to convince them. He repeated to them, over and over again, that it was impossible for Chlapowski to send him written orders, lest they should fall into the enemy's hands; besides, as the insurgents were unacquainted with the general's hand-writing, they could place no more dependence upon a written order than on the verbal one that had just been brought to them. It was in vain he endeavoured to convince them of the fatal consequences which their hesitation might bring on the national cause, as well as themselves; they were determined to wait, notwithstanding.

Prudence, even distrust, are sometimes necessary, particularly when the interests of a whole nation are at stake, which is to be rescued from the grasp of an ever-watchful enemy, who is constantly laying snares, and who knows well how to take advantage of the least fault. However, this prudence, this distrust must not proceed too far, for, in such case, favourable opportunities are liable to be lost, which, in war, are apt to be rather few and far between. It belongs to the man of experience and good judgment to decide when to act and when to forbear; when to advance and when to retreat; unfortunately, a great deal, too, depends on chance in these matters.

Evil counsels were about to prevail, and it was nearly decided to wait. But, fortunately, Parczewski, Emily Plater and others, who were personally acquainted with Zaleski, and who knew him incapable of treachery, thought otherwise, and defended their opinions so warmly, that it was concluded all at once to march. They took upon themselves the responsibility of this movement, and they were not deceived in their expectation, for they discovered the Polish Army, on the 6th of June, at Gabrielow, where the Prince Gabriel Oginski Matuszewicz, with the insurgents of Troki, and the students of Wilna, had already joined them.

What painter can depict, what poet can adequately describe a scene like this, when two people, who had been united by nature and sympathy, but whom violence had separated, were reunited after thirty-five years of constrained separation! The beauty and sublimity of such a spectacle is beyond the power of the pen to describe. Here all is noble and affecting. It is the uniting of two brothers, who have been separated from their cradle, to fight the common enemy, who has carried destruction and death into the bosom of the family around the paternal hearth. Once more united, they will be strong.

The standards are mingled, the banners are crossed, the white eagle of Poland is united to the knight of Lithuania, or rather, the two standards make but one, on which is written:

Let us die for freedom, and our country.

They embrace one another, arms are exchanged, hearts and tears commingle, a simultaneous shout, from ten thousand mouths, ascends to heaven. Heaven hears it, and the reunion is consummated. It is the shout of independence and fraternal feeling; of union against, and hatred for, their oppressors.

I was present, on that sublime occasion; I can therefore speak of it from personal knowledge. This day will always be remembered as one of the most solemn in my whole life. How beautiful was the spectacle of those two armies uniting to sustain the same struggle! I seem to myself to behold them, as they were then, proud and strong, full of youth and enthusiasm, interesting on account of the recollections of the past, and still more so by the victories foreboded by their fraternal union.

Often do I recall to memory those glorious and delightful moments, when everything smiled on our cause, and everyone was dreaming of victory. And I do still dream of victory, even as I did then; but I can scarcely express my feelings further. Being under the necessity of using a foreign language, I feel the want of suitable expressions for conveying a just idea of the true Polish feeling, which pervades my mind and soul.

Joy and hilarity predominate in all the camp. Everywhere the Lithuanians are seen mingling with the Poles, and the long evenings are spent in cheerfulness, and unrestrained conversations. The Lithuanians relate to the Poles all the troubles they have undergone, all the dangers they have been exposed to, through the delay of the Poles, and the hopeless situation from which they have been extricated by the arrival of their brethren, their saviours. The Poles, on the other hand, speak of the 29th of November, of the Battles of Grochow and Dembe; they relate to us prodigies of valour and devotedness. They mention the impatience of the nation to fly to the assistance of the Lithuanians, and they boldly expressed impatience, which the men in power in vain attempted to suppress.

They would then speculate on their new hopes and new projects, and on that futurity which, to those ardent youth and patriotic warriors, seemed so smiling. The whole country soon assumed a warlike aspect. Nothing was heard, during the day, but the clashing of arms in the hands of the insurgents, whom the old soldiers were drilling. In the evening, the Polish war songs,—the warlike *Mazourek the Chlopicki*, the simple and merry little song of *Krakus*, and the solemn hymn. *Honour to Poland*,—resounded in the air which heretofore had alone echoed the plaintive and monotonous chant of the Lithuanian serfs. The call of the vigilant sentinel would now and then interrupt the silence of the night. Everyone was in motion in the country, as well as in the camp. Joy filled all hearts, and hope sparkled in every eye— hope too sanguine, indeed, not to be disappointed; joy too violent to last long.

While the soldiers were giving themselves up to their joyous mood and military exercises, while awaiting the days of strife, the Polish general, with the principal chiefs of the insurrection, were considering how to make the best use of their local advantages, and the general plan of the Campaign; resolving to risk as little as possible, and, at the same time, to contest the ground inch by inch, and hand to hand.

The Prince Gabriel Oginski was the first to show that spirit of disinterestedness which ought to influence every true patriot, by surrendering his command to General Chlapowski; the other chiefs followed his example, and also resigned their power, with more eagerness than ambitious men generally exhibit in seizing it. "We devote our fortunes and our lives," said they in their address of June the 10th, "and, in return, we neither ask glory, titles nor rewards; all we want is to fulfil those duties which belong equally to every Pole, and which the long sufferings and the wants of our country require at our hands."

Chlapowski, after this address, thanked them, in the name of Poland, for all the Lithuanians had done to that time, for the common cause. He then organised his troops and appointed, as officers over them, old experienced military men, distributed arms among them, and gave to the several chiefs, such appointments as he thought they were entitled to, by their respective merits and capacity.

Emily Plater, whose fame had reached Poland, and which was spread, indeed, all over Europe, was an object of particular attention, on the part of the Polish general. As a woman, she was entitled to that consideration which is due to the sex; as a soldier, she was deserving of the esteem and admiration of her compatriots; besides, her devotedness was of a kind altogether too extraordinary to escape the particular notice of the chiefs.

The army saw, in her, one of those sublime beings which nature sometimes produces, as glorious ornaments to the human race; and the bards of the camp, inspired by her presence, would sing the exploits of the Joan d'Arc of Poland. Chlapowski welcomed her in a most flattering manner, but unwilling to see her precious life exposed to the dangers of the field, advised her to quit the army and rest from her fatigues; and inasmuch as the war, in consequence of the arrival of the regular troops, would assume, altogether, a new and regular system, she could with difficulty use, to advantage, the talents she had displayed during the insurrection, and she would be lost among the crowd of subaltern officers with which the army was well supplied.

The observations of the general were correct, but, woman and Pole as she was, Emily persisted in her design, and earnestly requested to be admitted into the ranks, she said:

As long as Poland is not entirely free, my vocation is that of a soldier, and as I am espoused to the cause of my country, without any ambitious views, I will not abandon it at a moment when dangers are more threatening, and battles more decisive.

She was appointed captain, commanding the first company of the first Lithuanian regiment, which, a few days after, was known as the twenty-fifth of the line.

At the same time the news was received that General Gielgud, with a Polish Army, had crossed the Niemen, and just entered Lithuania. This reinforcement seemed to add a great deal to the chance of success, but, in accordance with that fatality which has always pursued

Poland, it served merely to destroy the cause of freedom, by disseminating discord among the generals, and exciting their petty jealousies.

It was remarked from the first, that Chlapowski did not receive this news with much satisfaction; he seemed rather vexed than pleased, and it was in vain that he endeavoured to hide his vexation. Notwithstanding his patriotism, he was far from being free from personal ambition. The wish to shine and fill the pages of our history with his fame, was the principal motive of his actions, and he saw in the Polish revolution, not only the delivering of his country, but also the means of acquiring fame. When appointed by the general in chief, the commanding officer of the expedition into Lithuania, he accepted the appointment with the greatest eagerness, notwithstanding the small number of troops placed under his command.

He feared no dangers, and already thought himself the liberator of the invaded provinces, and as such, that his name would descend to posterity. This ambition, until this time laudable enough, led him to display all the resources of his talents; and the first step in his career being rather successful, seemed to justify the anticipation of a termination corresponding to it. The arrival of Gielgud deranged all his plans. As this officer was his superior in rank, he would, of course, be obliged to relinquish the command to him, and everything would be done under the name of Gielgud; and on this officer would be reflected all the glory of successful operations, while the name of Chlapowski, if mentioned at all, would come in as second to that of Gielgud, or, perhaps even would be confounded with those of the crowd of officers whose duty it is merely to execute the orders received from their superiors.

This idea was revolting to him, and his zeal began to abate. He now acted with unwillingness and reluctance, and too weak to sacrifice his personal interests to his country, he sacrificed Poland to the satisfaction of mortifying the man he considered his rival.

On the other hand, Gielgud was a most unfit person to command an expedition of such vast importance—an expedition, the result of which must have a powerful, as well as immediate influence, upon the fate of Poland. His corps, after the Battle of Ostrolenka, cut off from the rest of the army, was obliged to pass into Lithuania, and brought with it despondency, insubordination, and that dejection of mind so common to troops in such circumstances; troops, too, who entertained more contempt for, than confidence in, their chief. Gielgud did not attempt to repress this moral disorganisation;—he trusted to chance.

He was the son of one of the confederates of Targowiça, whose odious plot, in 1792, brought on the second dismemberment of Poland, and destroyed all the advantages of the constitution of the 3rd of May. A favourite with the Grand Duke Constantine, his patriotism could not be undoubted. Besides, he was too insignificant himself to inspire his compatriots, the Lithuanians, with much confidence. Gielgud had also some ambition of his own, but it was as pitiful as his own soul, and as base as his character. Glory and posterity possessed but a moderate share of his' admiration. All human greatness, in his estimation, consists in personal honours, and these, therefore, were the objects of his wishes. The title of commander in chief of a separate corps was enough to intoxicate him.

The honours he received, on his entry into Lithuania, completely turned his head, and, treated as a great man by the whim of fortune, he really thought himself such. Advice wounded his vanity, and he rejected it with arrogance. It was in vain the superior officers represented and urged that, in their actual situation, everything depended upon readiness of decision and action; he nevertheless followed his own way. It seemed as if he had no other object in view than the enjoyment of the dignity chance had thrown in his way, for he spent all his time in feasts and pleasures.

This incapacity and indifference of one of the generals, and the lukewarmness manifested by the other, ruined the cause of the insurrection, just at the moment it seemed to have gained stability. The Russians, who were then dispersed all over Lithuania in pursuit of the insurgents, and in that situation too weak to oppose the united forces of the insurgents, availed themselves of this inaction, on the part of our troops, to concentrate their own forces. Gen. Diebitsch, being informed of the arrival of the Poles, sent Gen. Kourouta, who, at the same time with Tosltoi, advanced, by forced marches, to the relief of Wilna.

It was then the shout of indignation, raised by the whole army, recalled Gen. Gielgud to his duty. The favourable moment had passed; Wilna, whose garrison before consisted of only three thousand men, had now, within its limits, thirty thousand men, well entrenched and actively employed in preparing for its defence.

Gielgud did not hesitate to offer them battle under the very walls of the city; they accepted the challenge, and the fight was a bloody one. The Polish troops worthily sustained their reputation, but the want of order and discipline neutralized their bravery and heroism.

Knowing that they had to deal with Russians, and that their freedom and country were at stake, they rushed with impetuosity on the masses of the enemy; and their efforts would, of necessity, have been crowned with success, had they been better guided. But what is courage without discipline? An heroic death, seldom victory, is the natural result.

This battle, which we ought to add decided nothing, afforded to the Russians an example of the impetuous courage of the Poles; but it also revealed to them the inferiority of their generals as well as the weak points of their army. Emboldened by this first advantage, and relying on the want of discipline of their adversaries, the Russians resumed the offensive, and compelled Gielgud to recede daily. Notwithstanding the promise extorted from the commander in chief, Emily was not present at the battle of Wilna. She was obliged to follow her regiment to Kowno, an important post situated at the confluence of the Wilna and the Niemen, and which was to serve as a point through which communication might be effected between Poland and the insurgents of the Palatinate of Augoustow.

In the rank of captain, which the commander in chief had conferred on her, Emily saw but the means of being useful to her country; she therefore applied herself to the study of military tactics, and patiently bore the heat of a burning day in June, as well as the chill of nights. She was a model to her men, and the object of their admiration. She seemed endowed with supernatural strength, when all in her was the effect of energy and firm resolve: her frail and delicate health was greatly impaired.

Unfortunate woman! thrown as she was into the midst of dangers and fatigues, she, whom nature had destined for the luxury of the *boudoir*, totally unmindful, as she was, of the comforts of life, she soon experienced the dire effects of her military life upon her delicate constitution. But she was never heard to utter a single word of dissatisfaction, or the least murmur of complaint. She was resolved to abide by all the consequences of the war. She ever kept herself actively employed, and worked as hard as if it had been her inevitable destiny. The first company, the men of which being just arrived, were yet in the freshness of their ardour and patriotism, soon became the choice company of the regiment.

When the news of the defeat of the Poles, before Wilna, reached Kowno, the troops, whose confidence in the Poles was almost enthusiastic, were disheartened. It seemed to them that such troops ought to be invincible, and, to Emily, it gave an overwhelming blow. It seemed to her that a thunderbolt had struck the cause of the insurgents to the heart, and that this defeat would disgrace the Polish name. Nevertheless, she succeeded in overcoming her grief; and by palliating the faults of the generals, extenuating the loss of the army as much as possible, and attributing Gielgud's precipitate retreat to certain manoeuvres designed to draw the Russians out of their entrenchments, she succeeded in restoring the courage of her men; but within herself, she felt sad and gloomy, and was consumed with her silent suffering and her own discouragements.

Alas! was such a holy cause, commenced under such auspices, to miscarry through the incapacity of its commanders? The future freedom of the country, her own future well-being, (for was not her very life identified with the cause she had espoused?) were to be thus prostrated;—and then she would lament her absence from the battle. "At least," would she say, "death would have been far preferable to defeat, and I would sooner have died than yield." But she was soon roused from these reflections by the imminent danger of that death which she was regretting the not having hazarded.

After the Battle of Wilna, the Russians, as we have already mentioned, assumed the offensive, and hotly pursued the Poles. Kowno, which as before observed was by its position an important point with regard to the plan of operations Gen. Gielgud had adopted, must of necessity have attracted the attention of the Russian commander;—the garrison being weak, the place could be carried by a bold onset.

Provided with this information, Tolstoi sent, on the 25th June, a pretty strong detachment before the city.

Col. Kiekiernicki, who commanded the place, unfortunately thought proper to disregard the intelligence, which came to him from every direction, and never even thought of blowing up the bridge over the Wilna, which offered an easy ingress to the enemy. This was an error! The colonel, with a weak regiment of badly armed conscripts, with scarcely a hundred horse, could hardly expect to withstand the attack of the Russians.

This imprudent conduct, on the part of Col. Kiekiernicki, was attended with fatal consequences, not only to himself, but also to the whole army; for it caused the total loss of the regiment Gielgud had confided to him.

The enemy, once in possession of the bridge, crossed the river without meeting an obstacle, and rushed at once on the weak columns of the Poles, which they overcome without difficulty. Overwhelmed by numbers and by the artillery, the 25th of the line began to give way; now the ranks are all disorder, the confusion increases, cartridges are exhausted, and our men, deprived of all the means of resistance, either allow themselves to be butchered by the Russians, or seek safety in flight.

Stationed on the right of the line, Emily Plater maintained her position with her company; she received the charge of the Russians with unflinching firmness; but as the artillery thinned her ranks more and more, she was, at last, forced to retreat. This intrepid heroine gave not up until the last, and she made the enemy pay dearly for every inch of ground they gained upon her; they fought almost hand to hand.

Her regiment was nearly all shot down, hardly one-third of it remaining and although surrounded by the Russians on all sides, yet she continued to fight; but it is no longer for victory nor to break through the battalions of Cossacks that she rushed into the midst of them, in defiance of a thousand deaths; it is to avoid falling alive into the hands of the Russians; she wished to leave them nothing but her dead body.

Kiekiernicki, the first cause of this bloody slaughter, being closely pursued by the Russians, arrived at the place where our heroine had been so long holding out in such an unequal contest. As soon as he perceived her, he cleared his way to her through the ranks of the enemy, and offering her his horse, entreats her to save a life so precious to the army, and at least, spare him the grief of her death. She refused him, but seemed uncertain how to decide for herself.

Overcome, at length, by the entreaties of the colonel, and the solicitations of her men, who had formed a fence around her with their own bodies, she retired. It was quite time she did so; her strength being so exhausted as to render her unable to stand any longer; her sword fell from her grasp, she could no longer offer any resistance. But, at last, making a final effort, she gathered her remaining strength, and rushing with a shout into the midst of the Cossacks, she cuts and thrusts, and at length succeeds in opening for herself a path through them, which she covers with their bodies.

But while she was escaping from the Russians, Col. Kiekiernicki was falling into their power, with the sweet consolation of having performed an act worthy of an honest man and a loyal soldier.

Having so miraculously escaped the bloody affair of Kowno, Emily repaired to Rosienie, where the broken remains of the 25th of the line had received orders to rendezvous, and replenish its ranks from the insurgents of Samogitia.

Chapter 13

Battles of Schawlé and Schawlany

It is not my intention to follow the Polish Generals in Lithuania; I shall speak of their disastrous campaign, only so far as its events may have any relation to the life of the heroine, whose biography I am now writing. Others will narrate these events, and pass judgment on the errors of Gielgud and Chlapowski; errors so numerous and glaring, that history alone can decide whether they were the result of incapacity or treason. Whatever may be that judgment, we may safely assert, that, from this very day, all the chiefs of the Polish Army in Lithuania, incurred nothing but shame and ignominy. They demoralised and disorganised this army by unaccountable delays and losses of time; and they harassed it by marches and counter-marches, which were as useless as they were numerous. They seemed to have no particular object in view, and to trust everything to chance.

Disorder prevailed in the ranks, without the least effort on their part to repress it; and, moreover, the culpable inertness of the central government, arbitrarily established by Gielgud, without the concurrence or consent of the Lithuanians, paralyzed the whole expedition, and rendered unavailable all the resources which the devotedness and patriotism of the invaded provinces might, otherwise, have afforded. The arrival of the Polish general into Lithuania gave the fatal blow to the insurrection. He called in all the detachments, and incorporated them into the old regiments, as if thousands of men could be transformed into properly drilled soldiers by a single dash of the pen.

By this measure, which necessity even cannot justify, and the fatal consequences of which the chiefs of the insurrection frankly warned him, Gielgud added another cause of disorder to those already existing in the army, and moreover left the country opened and exposed to the vengeance of the Russians, as well as to the dreadful effects of a reaction. The Russians had not now to contend with a force spread over the entire surface of the country; all they had to do was to complete the destruction of the remains of an army which was weak and isolated, lacking all kinds of munitions, and commanded by a chief destitute of the necessary talents.

The citizens of Lithuania, deserted by their protectors, wavered between the fear of persecution and their duties as patriots. Had patriotism prevailed with them, they did not know on whom to depend. They were endeavouring to find means of being useful to the cause of independence, but could see no possible way to effect their purpose. Surrounded, on all sides, by hostile armies, stripped of everything, and perceiving no prospect of victory, or even a chance for safety, the army was fast losing whatever discipline yet remained to it.

It was indeed a body undergoing decomposition, and which the least collision must destroy. The chiefs themselves were ignorant of the movements of the enemy, and took no trouble whatever to obtain information. Their capacity being totally inadequate to the duties of the important charge committed to them, they despaired of that sublime cause of freedom which, we must add, they never understood, and left the decision entirely to chance.

The patriots, seeing the turn which affairs had taken, deeply lamented the fate of their country, their past disasters, as well as those greater ones which they clearly saw were impending. Having no confidence in their generals, they foresaw no possibility of being extricated from their painful situation, and abandoned themselves to despair.— For a long time they indulged the hope that the command would be given up to Chlapowski; but owing to his ridiculous disinterestedness, they were deceived in their expectations. He wanted to make a show of subordination, while in fact, at the bottom of his heart, this office was the climax of his ambition. Besides, had this change been effected, it would have been, to the army, a change of names merely, for, as the sequel proved, Gielgud was almost as good as Chlapowski.

Emily's noble and generous heart bled at the sight of her country's calamities, and the deep sorrow caused by these misfortunes, affected her frail and delicate health more sensibly, even, than the fatigues which she had undergone. Placed by her rank in the army, in an inferior position, she could exert no influence whatever upon the method of conducting the war, and all she could do was to bewail the fate of her country.

Her only solace was the reflection that she should not survive it;

for she never, for a moment, entertained the idea of seeking refuge in a foreign clime, where the compassion of its inhabitants might afford her protection. Although in a complete state of despair, she yet remained faithful to her country in the day of its calamities. She even felt an enthusiastic attachment to it, and continued to discharge her duties with the same punctuality, and to take care of the company which remained under her command, with the same zeal as before, and this, too, with the overwhelming conviction that all that she could do was then useless, and that nothing could extricate Gen. Gielgud from the difficulties in which his unmannerly stubbornness had involved him.

The affair of Schawlé, in giving the last blow to the Polish Army, completed, in a suitable manner, the series of blunders (if I may use so mild an expression) which signalised the campaign in Lithuania. Gielgud, whom the Russians were chasing, not knowing which way to turn, conceived the mad idea (God knows why) of assaulting Schawlé, a little paltry town, which it has pleased the Lithuanians to adorn with the pompous name of *city*, and which is, in fact, nothing but an assemblage of a few miserable huts almost in ruins.

✶✶✶✶✶✶

"God knows why" is the expression used by Chlapowski, at that time chief of the staff: "We took up the line of march in order to attack Schawlé, *Dieu sait pourqiioi!*" See his letters on the military events of Poland and Lithuania, Berlin, 1834.

✶✶✶✶✶✶

At that place, in an entrenchment hastily thrown up, was a detachment of three thousand Russians, who, in all probability, could not long have withstood the attacks of the Poles, who were five times that number. The result unfortunately proved the contrary. Generals Gielgud and Chlapowski, who were conjointly the commanders during the battle, saw themselves completely beaten. Not only was the city not taken, but our ranks were horribly thinned; and our ammunition, which it was highly essential to be sparing of, was entirely exhausted.

The 25th of the line, after the disastrous affair of Kowno, had been sent to escort the baggage of the army to Schawlé, through another route; but, by some fatality attached to that regiment, they fell into an ambush which the Russians had set in the vicinity of Schawlany. The unavoidable disaster attending an unexpected attack in a narrow road, and in the midst of a dense forest, was greatly increased by the confusion of wagons, and the horses becoming unmanageable.

Notwithstanding these disadvantages, they made an intrepid defence, and came off with the loss, merely, of a considerable portion of the baggage, which, in fact, they cared but little for. After the conflict was over, the commanding officer could not find over a hundred men of his whole regiment. The rest, who were, for the most part, new recruits, had improved this opportunity to desert their colours. He brought them back, towards evening, to the vicinity of the village of Kourszany, where he found the army resting after its discomfiture. In Gen. Gielgud's report of the engagement in the forest, he compliments Capt. Emily Plater on her great courage and intrepidity, as well as her astonishing coolness amidst the most imminent dangers.

The infamous conduct of the commander in chief of the army could no longer be overlooked. It was no longer possible for him to retain the command, as he had become the object of execration, not only to the officers, but also to every private in the army, by whom he was openly called the author of all our disasters, and some even went so far as to accuse him of treason.

The critical situation in which we were placed, rendered it highly necessary to call a council of war. This was convoked on the next night, and after a long discussion on the means of saving the army, it was finally resolved to retreat into Poland.

Gielgud, in consequence of this decision, lost his command; the army was divided into three separate corps, and the command of each confided to Gen. Chlapowski, Rohland and Dembinski, who were to act separately, the better to enable them to effect a passage over the Niemen.

As soon as the order was promulgated, each one prepared himself to follow the general who most fully possessed his confidence. The fictitious confidence attached to the name of Gen. Chlapowski, although much diminished by the inactivity and indifference which he had displayed, while chief of Gielgud's staff, induced almost every one to believe that he, alone, could effect that retreat as skilfully as he had, six weeks before, effected his entrance into Lithuania, by means as bold as they were ingenious. Consequently, the greatest part placed themselves under his command; and Emily Plater, whose regiment no longer existed, sharing in this opinion, or rather the general error, joined and followed him.

The general confidence reposed in the talents of Chlapowski would not allow them, for a moment, to doubt a successful return into Poland, where everyone hoped to clear himself of the disgrace with which Gielgud had covered the whole army. They were all ready to make any sacrifice for the attainment of this object. The burning of the baggage excited but a slight murmur. They considered as nothing their continual marches and want of food and rest; the anticipation of rejoining the standards of their brethren alone constituted their support and consolation.

We had thus proceeded by forced marches, for two days and two nights, without meeting a single enemy, and we began to hope that he had lost all traces of us, and that soon our wishes would be realised, when, toward the beginning of the third day, we descried the boundaries of Prussia. We halted, and Chlapowski then informed us, that for us to reach Poland in safety was impracticable, and that he thought it his duty to take advantage of the only chance of safety remaining to us, namely the protection of Prussia.

It would be difficult indeed to give an idea of the effect which this unexpected decision produced in the army, and of the consternation which pervaded it. To lay down those arms, the sole dependence of our dearest hopes; to surrender ourselves, of our own free will and accord, prisoners to a power which, although neutral, was yet hostile to our cause, and thus see Prussia triumph over us; to rot in inaction when our country was in danger and required all the efforts of her sons to help her; to lead a wretched life in shame and disgrace; to have to blush before the stranger as well as our compatriots, who would brand us with cowardice and perhaps treason,—how exasperating were such considerations! How distressing such prospects to a Pole!

But if, on the one hand, honour revolted at such an ignominious retreat, on the other, the imagination, struck with such a frightful picture of our situation, a picture shaded with its own sombre hues, represented the return into Poland as impracticable or as impossible. It is not to be wondered at, then, that the greatest part of the army, though with hearts bursting with grief and shame, followed the general into the Prussian territory; and yet some, who were endowed with a most energetic spirit and heroic courage, rushed headlong amid the Russians, with a faint expectation of forcing their way through them into Poland, and thus being yet able to serve the cause of independence.

Emily Plater, who was not surpassed in courage and patriotism by anyone, experienced, throughout, these feelings in common with her companions in arms, but in a greater degree; for, being a woman, she loved her country as a woman knows how to love, having fought for it with the most manly courage. Her noble and enthusiastic soul had but one wish, and that was to save her country, or to die for it, should it become necessary. With her the sacrifice was as sincere as it was entire. She could not bring herself to believe that all was lost beyond hope. She was neither dejected nor discouraged. The love of country afforded her the needful strength to bear the weight of misfortunes which overwhelmed us. Her firm conviction of the justice of our cause nourished hope in her own heart.

During the whole of this retreat, she appeared calm and resigned, hoping for better days, and feeding her imagination with heroic projects. Often, she would deem herself in Poland, making her entrance into Warsaw, whence she was assisting, as it seemed to her, to expel the Russians, when a report reached her that she was to finish all her dreams in Prussia.

At first, she refused to believe a word of it, and ran to Chlapowski to ascertain the truth of it. At the first words of the general, she resigned all hope, and the truth appeared before her eyes in all its gloomy horror. Then, a sublime scene took place in Chlapowski's tent. A female, weak and timid, though strong in patriotism, and as full of hatred for the Russians as she was of contempt for cowards and traitors, dared to face him, and reproach him with his base, ignominious conduct. She said to him:

> You have betrayed the confidence reposed in you, you have betrayed the cause of freedom and of our country, as well as of honour. As for myself, I will not follow your steps into a foreign country to expose my shame to strangers. Some blood yet remains in my veins, and I have still left an arm to raise the sword against the enemy. I have a proud heart, too, which never will submit to the ignominy of treason. Go to Prussia! Your representation of our situation does not affright me. I prefer a thousand deaths to dishonour, and I fear not to encounter them while forcing my way through the Russian battalions, in order to go and offer to my country this sword, which I have already raised in her defence, and the sacrifice of my life, if necessary.

As soon as she had left the general's tent, she collected her friends, and communicated to them the scene which had just taken place, and, also, the unalterable resolution which she had taken. Death, in the most frightful shape, appeared to her preferable to infamy. She, therefore, lost not a moment. The same evening, she left the army, accompanied by her indispensable friend Mary Raszanowicz, and Count

Caesar Plater, who wished to share her dangers as well as her glory.

The next day. Gen. Chlapowski gave up his sword to the Prussian authorities, who were astonished to see a Pole lay down his arms.

CHAPTER 14

Her Death

Ten days after this event, three persons might be seen reclining upon a knoll, surrounded by a marsh and the thick forests of Augustin. They are clad in the common dress of the peasants of the country. They have on coarse linen frocks, and their feet are covered with sandals of bark. But their noble and delicate features betray their real station; and those arms, carefully concealed under their garments, show that they belong to the remains of the Lithuanian army, which the Russians are everywhere in pursuit of. They seem to be impatiently and anxiously waiting for someone, although a profound silence prevails among them, and they are startled at the least noise.

"Cover your arms, Emily," says one of them in a low voice, "the air is damp and we have but little powder." These are the only words which are uttered during a long and fruitless expectation of three or four hours.

How deeply affecting is the spectacle of these noble children of Poland, concealed in the thickets, in the midst of hostile battalions, and who are thus encountering hardships, death and slavery, in order to join the battles of their country, and serve her to the last!

Sublime patriotism! Unquenchable flame, which, like the magnetic force in the natural world, animates the soul, and endues it with power to execute things which are seemingly beyond the limit of human achievement! Glorious sentiments of devotedness, ready for any sacrifice, regardless of danger and suffering, how worthy of our deep respect and admiration; and how pitiful the soul which cannot understand you!

The sun was beginning to decline, the woods re-echoed the lowings of the flocks, which were leaving their pasture, and the plaintive and monotonous song of the herdsman, who was leading them back to the village. The evening was dark and cloudy; very soon, a cold fine rain set in; the young people wrapped themselves up as well as they were able in their miserable frocks, but they did not dare to leave their retreats in order to go to seek shelter in some cottage.

"How slow in returning !" said the youngest of the three, smiling.

"Have no fear, Mary," was the reply, "our guide is a Samogitian, and the faith of the Samogitians has been well proved. Some obstacle, without doubt, has detained him beyond the appointed hour, but he will soon return, and I hope we shall resume our journey tonight."

"That is if he brings us something to eat," said Mary; "for it is now twenty-four hours since we partook of food, and I feel that I have great need of refreshment."

"Have courage ladies," said Caesar Plater, smiling, "and our misfortunes will soon be ended. Our journey, as you well know, has been thus far difficult and disagreeable, but the most difficult part of it has been accomplished. Thank God and the brave peasants of Samogitia, we have passed the Niemen, that barrier which separated us from Poland, and in a few days, I hope, we shall be in Warsaw."

"A few days yet," repeated Emily, casting a look of the deepest sadness upon her limbs, which were bruised and torn by a long journey through marshes and dense forests, and which seemed to refuse to bear her further. The train of sorrowful thoughts which was passing through her mind was interrupted by a sharp and prolonged whistle, and a peasant, about sixty years of age, but still fresh and vigorous, was seen approaching.

"God be thanked, my children," said he to them, I am somewhat late, but it has been impossible for me to arrive sooner. These Russian dogs seized me, as I was coming out of the wood, and I have passed a very bad quarter of an hour in the hands of these brigands. They were a long time searching me and asking me questions. Fortunately, I belong to the country, and am well known, thank God! So, the whole village confirmed my statement, when I told them that I was going to the neighbouring village to see my father-in-law, Martin the blacksmith. At last they let me go, and I came off with only a few blows, which God, in his own good time, will, without doubt, return to them."

"The infamous villains !" cried Mary.

"In the meanwhile, I have brought you something to eat and I am very sure you must have great need of it;" and at the same time, he drew from his wallet a black loaf, half bran, a piece of cheese, hard as a stone, and a small bottle of brandy. "All this is not worth much; but it will, nevertheless, serve to appease hunger in some degree. God knows I feared to take anything more, for fear of exciting the suspicion of these Russians."

"This is better than nothing," said Mary, gayly, and she began to eat with apparent appetite.

"What news, old man ?" asked Count Plater. "Can we soon renew our march?"

"Impossible yet, my good sir; the country is full of Russians, who are in pursuit of our brave Pouschet. We must wait until this rabble quits the country, or at least until sleep closes their eyes, so that you may pass, with safety, through these files of Cossacks. In the meanwhile, take some rest; sleep, and I will awaken you when it will be safe for you to commence your journey."

Emily took but little nourishment. For several days, a burning fever had consumed her. The blood boiled in her veins, and her hot breath had rendered her lips parched. Her heavy head fell back upon her shoulders, and she felt within her the germ of a malady, which she knew would not permit her to pursue her projects, and witness the accomplishment of her beautiful dreams. She concealed, in the meanwhile, her frightful condition from the unfortunate companions of her journey, and passed whole nights in prayer to God that he would grant her, at least, one thing; that she might behold Warsaw—might see the Polish standard, and then die. Long before daylight, the old man called up our pilgrims, and told them it was time to set out. He enjoined on them the most profound silence, and recommended the utmost precaution until they should have passed the Russian camp, along which they had to pass.

The young people followed their guide in deep silence, hardly venturing to breathe. Thanks to their precautions and the darkness of the night, they succeeded in winding round the camp without alarming the sentinels, whose calls they distinctly heard. Although she felt her illness increase continually, Emily kept up her march, repressing with the greatest care all expression of pain. Fever was consuming her, but still, notwithstanding her lacerated feet, she still continued to advance. The strength of the spirit exceeded that of the body. Patriotism, alone, helped to sustain her, but at last she was obliged to give up. All at once, her sight became dim, her limbs refused to perform their office longer, and she at length fainted.

"Great God!" ejaculated the old man. "Take up your brother, my children, and carry him where I will show you; the Russians will not seek him there."

Mary Raszanowicz and the Count Plater took Emily in their arms, and in about a quarter of an hour the mournful train stopped before the door of a miserable looking hut. It was that of the forester.

During this unhappy war, it was not a rare sight to see insurgents pursued by the Russians, or indeed citizens flying before persecution, soliciting shelter from the peasants, which was always most eagerly granted.

The arrival, therefore, of these four persons did not astonish the peaceable inhabitants of this poor cottage. The old man entered first, exchanged a few words in Samogitian with the forester and his wife, who instantly arose to furnish aid to the sick one. They placed the cold and pallid body of Emily upon a bed and covered it up warmly, and sought to recall it , to life, for she had not yet recovered her sensibility. It was a body in which death and life were sustaining a fierce struggle for the mastery.

"Blessed Jesus!" exclaimed the forester's wife, as she was bathing Emily's temples with brandy; "so young and already so unfortunate! Poor child, he has suffered much."

"May the curse of heaven fall upon the *Tzar*," answered the peasants.

All at once, the woman raised a shriek, which neither Caesar nor Mary understood the reason of—In her efforts to reanimate Emily she had discovered her sex, and the idea immediately occurred to her, that this person could be no other than the Countess Emily Plater, whose exploits she had often heard praised. Admiration and astonishment rendered her, for a moment, mute and motionless.

She stared, in mute contemplation, upon the thin and pale face of the dying Emily. She took her husband aside, and communicated to him the curious discovery which she had made, but which she would not make known to any other individual so long as Emily lived.

They had relinquished all hope of restoring her, when a sudden and convulsive chill pervaded her frame. She then opened her eyes, and perceiving herself in a hut, surrounded by her fellow travellers, her fainting fit in the forest came to her recollection, and pressing the hand of her cousin, said to him, not without effort:

"My strength is failing me; I feel that death is not far distant. Continue your journey.—May you reach Warsaw in safety;—you may be able to render, there, some service to our country. As for me, my career is ended. Grieve no more for poor Emily, she well knows how to die."

Caesar Plater, alarmed at the danger of his cousin, whose state of health was not yet removed from danger, and not wishing to leave her in the cottage of the forester, whose extreme poverty, notwithstanding his good will and tenderness of feeling, would forbid his bestowing upon her the extreme care which her situation required, applied to the proprietor of the village, and explaining to him the whole mystery, entreated him to lend his assistance to a dying female, exhausted by fatigue, and whose unbounded and exalted devotedness to the Polish cause, had placed her in this situation.

Citizen A—— was a good patriot, and, above all, an honest man; he granted his request at once, and the poor patient was carried to his house, where she received medical attendance, and the most assiduous and tender care.

Relieved from his extreme anxiety, with respect to Emily, Caesar Plater resumed his journey, and in a short time arrived at Warsaw. We cannot help devoting here a few words to this young hero of Poland, who himself also was a remarkable instance of self-devotion to his country, and who sacrificed everything in her service. What has he not done for Poland? And what would he not have done in order to see her free and independent?

At the age of twenty-one, he forsook his rank and fortune to place himself at the head of the peasants whom he had excited to revolt, and furnished with arms. He fought as long as the contest lasted, and when all was lost in Lithuania, he repaired to Poland, where he still continued to fight, being always found in front, where duty called a true Pole. Most faithful in every duty, and devoted to the cause he had espoused, he rendered important services to that cause. All his property has been confiscated, and he himself proscribed.

But all this does not prevent him from serving his country, in being useful to the Polish cause in France, where he has sought refuge. The small amount he has saved from the wreck of his fortune, he devotes to the relief of those of his compatriots who are more unfortunate, even, than himself, and particularly to the education of the young emigrants, whose means are insufficient for preparing them, as true Poles, to bring back to their native country, at some future time, those arts and sciences which the Autocrat has taken so much pains to suppress.

Mary Raszanowicz, sacrificing glory to friendship, remained near the bed of sickness, and devoted herself day and night to the unremitted care of her, whose dangers and fatigues she had for so long time shared.

Quietness, and the skill of the physician, at last prevailed in saving Emily from the jaws of death, and she began to recover her strength in this hospitable mansion, where she was secreted under the name of Mademoiselle Korawinska, and constantly treated with all the respect she was entitled to, by her birth, devotedness and misfortunes.

Meanwhile, the state of affairs in Poland were taking a bad turn. Since the Battle of Ostrolenka, Skrzynecki was remaining in a state of the most unaccountable inaction. After the death of Diebitsch, Paskiewicz, who had been appointed to the command of the Russian Army, had effected, without any molestation, his passage over the Vistula.

The Poles, whom the seeming indifference of their general in chief had exasperated, and, who, probably, were too easily inclined to believe in the accusations of the discontented, deprived him of the command, without well knowing whom to appoint in his place. This important and delicate charge, which some refused, while others exercised it for a few days only, at last fell into the hands of Krukowiecki, an ambitious and intriguing man, and one in respect to whom the Poles ought to have been more on their guard than anyone else; the previous conduct of this chief having been far from a character to inspire favour and confidence. The army, which this continual change of commanders had actually demoralised, lost all sense of subordination; contradictory orders were issued, and, of course, badly executed.

There was no longer any union, or plan of action, and the orders issued one day, were countermanded the next. In the meanwhile, Paskiewicz drew near to Warsaw, and whether it was that Krukowiecki had already sold himself to the Russians, or whether he was destitute of all the qualities of a general, or whether the indifference of the chiefs had paralyzed the courage of the army; Warsaw surrendered, in pursuance of a capitulation between Krukowiecki and Paskiewicz.

After the loss of the capital, the army was by no means disposed to abandon the cause. It wished to contend as long as there was an inch of Polish ground remaining. But those in power had already become discouraged, and depression of mind succeeded to patriotism. They lost all confidence in their cause, discord arose among them, their minds became exasperated, they began to negotiate, and in conclusion, Rybinski. who had been lately appointed commander in chief of the Polish Army, marched the troops into the Prussian territory, and placed them under the protection of King William.

Such was the final result of this glorious struggle, which, during several months, had astonished all Europe, and kept it in suspense between hope and fear. The nations saw on one side, barbarity—hideous barbarity, with its hordes of brute and submissive savages, who, under the fear of the *knout* and the cannon's mouth were compelled to encounter death. On the other, a long oppressed and suffering nation, jealous of its rights, and who was desirous of recovering its independence.

A mere handful of brave men accomplished all that courage and patriotism could effect. But alas! they yielded, because Europe forsook them in their struggle,—heroic struggle, in which two nations eagerly fought hand to hand with each other,—bloody and glorious struggle, which preserved France from a third invasion, and inflicted a deep, and, perhaps, incurable wound upon the Russian colossus. Had it not been for this long and bloody fight for several months, on the banks of the Vistula, and under the walls of Warsaw, it is not improbable that the Russians might have invaded the world, and accomplished their gigantic project of universal empire. (A very extravagant idea, but such is the text. *Translator*).

Liberty would have been suppressed in every country in which it is a constituent element in the happiness of the people. Slavery and barbarity would have reigned everywhere supreme. Glory to my country! By her own death she has been the salvation of the world. All these events closely followed each other, and becoming known to the citizens of the distant provinces, destroyed their deeply cherished hopes. This sad news was kept with the most scrupulous care from the knowledge of Emily, in the apprehension that it would produce a relapse which might prove fatal. But all precaution proved fruitless. The overwhelming intelligence of the Poles having sought refuge in Prussia reached her ears, and gave her the fatal blow.

Her soul, identified with the existence of Poland, refused to inhabit longer its shattered tenement, worn out by fatigues and sufferings; and all that medical skill could possibly effect, was to prolong, for a few miserable days, an existence which had become hateful to her, since she had learned that Poland, her beloved country, had been enslaved again. She could not longer dwell on that soil, which had, once more, fallen into the possession of barbarians, who would overwhelm its enslaved inhabitants with woe.

Her heart was broken, and her noble soul disdained an existence which henceforth was to be replete with misery and suffering. She had no wish to live any longer; all her ties with this world were rent asunder, and, therefore, it was with feelings of gladness that she saw the

111

approach of death. Hardly anything in the world could have induced her to sacrifice the freedom of her own dear Poland, which, in her own imagination, she had so long considered free and happy, but now trampled under the feet of two hundred thousand Russians, and, like herself, breathing her last.

Feeling the approach of her last hour, after having submitted herself to God's holy will, and received the last consolations of religion, she asked for her arms. She seized them with a feeble grasp, and a burning tear escaped from her eyelid. Her look seemed for a moment to express regret. Alas! all she regretted and wept for, was that she had failed in saving her country, and that she was unable to serve that country longer. Unwilling to be separated from her arms, she requested that they might be placed in her tomb; and in the very act of pressing them close to her heart, she expired. Her last breath was a supplication to the Supreme Being, that He would vouchsafe to take under his holy protection her suffering compatriots, who, less fortunate than herself, remained exposed to the vengeful ire of their tyrants, as well as her unhappy country, which Heaven seemed to have forsaken.

Emily Plater expired on the 23rd day of December, 1831.—Such was the short but glorious career of this heroic female, who in the twenty-sixth year of her age, fell a victim to the misfortunes of her country. Endowed by nature with a masculine character and a sanguine temperament, she marked out for herself a lofty, bold and poetic destiny; and when the fit opportunity for realising her youthful dream occurred, she did not shrink from danger and fatigue, but always showed herself worthy of her self-imposed mission. Endowed with all those qualities, which render a woman almost an object of adoration, she was gentle, benevolent, susceptible of the enjoyment of friendship and feelings of gratitude, but always a perfect stranger to the emotions of love.

When she lost her mother, she bestowed her love exclusively upon her country. She clung to Poland with all the passionate ardour of a lover. Poland alone was the subject of her dreams, and she was ever ready to sacrifice her happiness, her own opinions, and life itself, to the independence of that country which she so passionately loved.

Having adopted Joan d'Arc for her model, she equalled that extraordinary woman in courage and devotedness; the only difference between them is, that the one met with success, and the other with misfortune; and yet both died the victims of their patriotism. Religious writers, in speaking of Joan d'Arc, have long sought to ascribe to a miracle, that which was purely the effect of religious enthusiasm, and entire devotedness to the cause of her country. What is it that an exalted patriotism cannot achieve! What is it that a being, even naturally so weak, is not capable of, when strongly impressed by noble and holy motives! Joan d'Arc, impelled by her religious enthusiasm, at the sight of the misfortunes of her country, which she believed herself destined to relieve, flies to the field.

On the other hand, Emily Plater, unable to behold any longer the sufferings of Poland in the chains of a cruel slavery, calls to arms her compatriots as soon as the first shout of independence is heard. They are two of the most beautiful and interesting beings the annals of any nation can offer. Joan d'Arc roused Charles VII. from his effeminate pleasures, and placed a sword in his hands to reconquer his kingdom, and expel the English from the soil.

Emily Plater electrified her compatriots, whom slavery had degraded. She rekindled, in every heart, the fire of patriotism and devotedness. Both were models, in their respective countries, worthy of imitation. But to assist the efforts of Joan d'Arc, the French had a well-appointed army; whereas the Lithuanians had only a few insurgents from the peasantry, badly equipped, and almost destitute of arms, and totally unacquainted with the use of the sword or musket.

It was not the fault of Emily Plater if we had no Dunois or La Trémouilles to assist her in her great undertakings. If the maid of Orleans is, to this day, the glory and pride of France, so will Emily Plater be the glory and pride of Poland, and her name will descend to posterity, blessed by the nation she has endeavoured to wrest from barbarity and oppression, and the admiration of all that possesses a manly heart.

Joan d'Arc and Emily Plater are two of the most resplendent jewels in the crown of nations. They are ornaments of humanity, and the nations who shall produce such persons will always rank among the first in the world. Good trees alone can produce such good fruit.

The obsequies of Emily Plater were simple and mournful. The whole country being in possession of the despot, how could those funeral solemnities, due to the heroine of our liberty, be performed! No funeral oration was pronounced over the grave. She was privately buried, like a precious relic, which they were endeavouring to preserve from the outrages and profanations of impious barbarians. A wooden cross only was placed at the head of her grave, which some time after was covered with a white stone slab, until the day shall arrive when her grateful country, in the enjoyment of freedom and glory, will be permitted to raise to her memory, a monument worthy of her and her distinguished services.

The only epitaph on that stone is the single word,

EMILIA.

To the Memory of the Countess

What is a woman's weak, delicate form,
But a flower that droops beneath every storm,—
That shrinks as the chilly breeze wanders by.
And if tempests arise must fade and die!
Oh! let her be placed on a fairy throne,
To be flattered, and worshipped, and gazed upon;
She never was destined to view the strife,
The carnage, the toil of this earthly life;
But to smile and charm in the summer hours,
Basking in sunshine like other sweet flow'rs.
Oh! never should sorrow its dim form rear,
To stain that cheek with its scalding tear.
For the radiant light of those sunny eyes,
Can only beam under cloudless skies;
And her fairy footsteps may only fall
In a bower of love, or the banquet hall.
Such woman was ever—and still must be—
No: Poland! e'en woman can change for thee:
She doth not shrink from the scathing storm,
Tho' fragile and weak be her lovely form;
She doth not desert in the hour of need
Her Country, her friends, but with them will bleed,
As a guardian spirit, will hover around
Where artillery thunders and trumpets sound.
And oh! if "the lion will turn and flee
From a maid in the pride of her purity,"
What demon could harm e'en a single hair
Of the angel forms that minister there?

Couronne Poétique.

ELEGIE.

Dors, o ma Pologne, dors en paix dans ce qu'ils appellent ta tombe ; moi, je sais que c'est ton berceau.

F. DE LAMENNAIS.

Passe à l'entour de moi, passe, léger fantôme ;
Qu'un peuple infortuné dans son exil me nomme,
    Mais qu'il me nomme avec orgueil !
Salut à toi, salut, vierge, auguste héroïne,
Jeanne d'Arc de la France ! oh ! quel front ne s'incline
    Devant ta vie et ton cercueil !
Ta vie ! elle est sublime ! ah ! que ton ame ardente
Devait souffrir de voir la Pologne mourante
    Et par les rois mise en lambeaux !
Ces voraces vautours, avec des cris de joie,
Se l'étaient partagée, et dormaient sur leur proie
    Qui reposait dans trois tombeaux.*

II.

Mais dans ces trois tombeaux courait encor la vie,

* La Pologne partagée entre la Russie, la Prusse et l'Autriche.

Il ne saurait mourir le feu qui vivifie ;
    Parfois seulement il s'endort,
Et les tyrans alors triomphent par le glaive :
    Le peuple esclave souffre et sert.
Mais leur règne est bien court ; la Liberté se lève
    Et brise leur sceptre de fer.

Oh ! que tu dus jouir, quand tu vis ta patrie,
    Tout-à-coup ansi se levant,
Comme un frêle roseau, briser la tyrannie
    Qui tremblait sur le sol mouvant !

Les tombeaux s'entr'ouvraient comme les tentes pleines
    D'un camp qui s'éveille au matin :
Des héros en sortaient.—Ils couvrirent les plaines,
    Comme des cavales sans frein.

Ils jetèrent au monde un cri d'indépendance
    Que voulaient-ils ? la Liberté,
Le plus beau des trésors.—Cinquante ans de souffrance
    Le leur avaient bien mérité.

Au milieu de leurs rangs tu t'élancas sans crainte,
    Comme un chevalier d'autrefois,
Appelant tout un peuple à la liberté sainte
    Et par l'exemple et par la voix.

Que n'aurais-tu pas fait pour briser les entraves
    Qui sur la Pologne pesaient,
Pour fouler à tes pieds ces bataillons d'esclaves
Qui sur son corps sanglant passaient et repassaient ?

III.

Tu combattis long-temps, Héroïne inspirée !
Mais, hélas ! la patrà ises tyrans livrée
    Redescendit dans son cercueil.

Ses frères, ses amis, qui devaient la défendre,
L'avaient abandonnée, et nous vîmes s'étendre
    Sur elle un long crêpe de deuil.

Elle tomba.—Posant leur main lourde sur elle,
Ses bourreaux, satisfaits dans leur rage cruelle,
    L'écrasent sous un joug pesant.
Oh ! qui jamais souffrit un plus cruel martyre ?
Attachée à sa croix, elle souffre, elle expire,
Et de ses flancs ouverts coulent des flots de sang.

Mais, par ces flots de sang, bienfaisante rosée,
La Pologne, ô mon Dieu ! sera fertilisée ;
    Elle enfantera des héros.

Et, comme un fier lion secouant sa crinière
Elle se lèvera puissante, libre et fière,
    Et dévorera ses bourreaux.
J'en jure par le Ciel, la Pologne qui tombe,
Comme autrefois le Christ, sortira de sa tombe,
    Brillante comme un glaive ardent.
Un peuple d'exilés reverra sa patrie ;
Ils fouleront aux pieds l'ignoble barbarie ;
    Ils broiront leurs sous la dent.

IV.

Et toi, Vierge martyre, alors qu'après ton rêve
    De patrie et de liberté,
Tu vis cette patrie expirer sous le glaive ;
    Quand son cadavre ensanglanté
Fut remis dans la tombe et scellé sous la pierre,
    Ah ! que ton grand cœur fut brisé !
Comme autrefois celui de Marie au Calvaire,
    De sept glaives il fut percé.
Tu t'offris au Seigneur toi-même en sacrifice.

Comme la fille de Jephté ;
Et tu cherchas au ciel, séjour de la justice,
La patrie et la liberté.

La patrie ! *** elle souffre ; innocente victime,
Vers le Ciel elle tend les bras,
Elle pleure, elle prie ***—et son tyran l'opprime,
Et le Ciel ne l'écoute pas !

Et dans ses champs déserts que couvrent les ruines,
L'étranger insulte à ses maux !
Elle porte à son front la couronne d'épines,
Sa chaste robe est en lambeaux,
Son sein est lacéré, son sang à flots ruisselle
Et se mêle aux pleurs des martyrs.

O vierge, dans le ciel invoque Dieu pour elle !
Offre son sang et ses soupirs
Au dieu des opprimés, au dieu de l'innocence !
Que l'aube perce enfin la nuit,
Entraînant sur ses pas le jour de la vengeance
Et la liberté qui la fuit !

Que l'étoile s'élève et plus grande et plus belle !
Qu'elle brille aux yeux des mortels !
Que ta Pologne, ô toi, Vierge morte pour elle,
Puisse t'élever des autels !

DIE GRAEFIN PLATER.

Es giebt ein gut, wer' s einmahl hat geschmecket
Der weiss von keinem lieblichern mehr dann ;
Verlieren kann all andres er ; doch strecket
Ein feind die hand nach diesem gut hinan ;
So wird zum zorn selbst sanftmuth aufgeschrecket,
Das milde weib wird hochempoert zum mann.
O freiheit, nimmermehr kann dich vergessen,
Du suesses gut, wer einmahl dich besessen.

Nach langen naechten war es tag geworden,
Es flohen vor dem neuen, ros' gen Licht
Zurueck die finsternissgebornen horden,
Und freie sahen frei' n ins angesicht.
Doch wieder draengt die alte nacht aus norden,
Sie goennt den neuen schoenen tag dir nicht.
Dem theuren gut will jedes herz sich weihen,
Auch eine jungfrau eilt mit in die reihen.

Den wie Johanna, als das land der Franken
Von fremder schaar mit untergann bedroht,
Begelstert eintrat in die blut' gen schranken,
Bis nicht die bringer mehr unwuerd' ger noth
Aus der Loire schoenen fluthen tranken :
So trieb des geistes stuermisches gebot
Die hohe jungfrau in den laerm der schlachten,

Und liess sie nicht der zarten glieder achten.

Jhr gold hat sie dem vaterland geschicket,
Mit rauhem zelt vertauscht ihr graeflich schloss;
Und wo der tod die reihen wild durchzuecket,
Da tummelt auch die jungfrau kuehn ihr ross.
Und manche tapfre that ist ihr gegluecket,
Oft floh vor frauenschwerd der feinde tross;
Nur dann erst legte sie das schlachtschwerdt nieder,
Als rings das schoene licht verdraenget wieder.

Du hohe maid im kriegerischer kleide!
Mit Saragossa's heldenmaedchen hast,
Und mit Johanna du ein gleich geschmeide,
Viel edler, als des golds, der perlen last.
Weint nun dein freies herz im tiesen leide,
Weil deiner heimath noth dich schmerzlich fasst;
So denk': noch muesste Polens morgen tagen,
Wenn, deinem gleich, jedwedes herz geschlagen!

Nur eines moegst du nimmermehr dir sagen,
Selbst das zu denken, waere gar zu graus!
Die geister derer, die im feld erschlagen,
Sie muessten aus der stillen gruft heraus,
Und rastlos angst, gewissensqualen tragen
Um mitternacht in des verruchten haus,
Wenn — o, nur der nicht von den freveln allen! —
Wenn Polen — — Polen durch v e r r a t h gefallen. —

Sulla Tomba

DI

EMILIA PLATER.

Sonetto.

Dal' bianco sasso che il gran cener serra
    Dell' augusta virago Litüana,
    Voce suonò che andrà di terra in terra,
    E fuor del Tempo viver à lontana.

Ti scuoti, o Europa, a fulminar la guerra
    Contro la turba de' tiranni insana,
    Ch'or piega al giogo, or con la scure atterra,
    Quasi vil gregge la famiglia umana!

Ti scuoti, o Europa, ed al mio amor t'accendi!
    E patrio amor c'ha sempiterno'l volo,
    Ed ha favilla di superna face.

Ti scuoti, o Europa, e da una donn apprendi,
    Che Patria e Libertade è un nome solo****
    E il sonno è vituperio, e non è Pace!

The Battle of Warsaw
6-7 September 1831

By A. S. Krause

Throughout the summer of 1831 the city of Warsaw lay like a city
of the dead. Its magnificent palaces appeared as though deserted; its
streets were lonesome, and the few who ventured from within their
dwellings moved about as though smitten.

Although not declared, Warsaw lay in a state of siege. The struggle
for liberty, long maintained by the brave nation of Poles, was drawing
to a close, and all felt that though hitherto victorious in the field, they
must fall before the countless hordes of Russia in the end.

There had been a rising in the previous year. Undeterred by the
knowledge that they were a handful against millions, and encouraged
by the recent examples of France and Belgium, the Poles of Warsaw
had risen in revolt against the despotism of Russia, as personified by
Constantine, the ferocious governor of their city.

The direct cause of the outbreak was, as is usual in such cases,
slight—a bogus trial on a popular officer for an imaginary offence.
A verdict contrary to the weight of evidence, a street row among the
military students, a dozen of whom were promptly flogged with the
knout, while others were imprisoned, and the mischief was done. The
young Poles rose in November, and without ceremony broke into the
prison and freed their comrades. The gates of the palace were forced,
and the'governor sought; but without success, he having escaped. But
while Constantine evaded the vengeance of his victims, his lieutenants
fared otherwise, and many of them fell into the hands of their relentless enemies. For the moment, the Polish capital was in the hands of
the Poles.

The Russian aristocracy disappeared, and at every street corner

123

meetings were held at which the proceedings were constantly interrupted by cries of "*Niech zyie Polska*"—Poland for ever! This state of things continued throughout the winter of 1830. The ice-bound *steppes* forbade the Russians taking action. But the *Czar* vowed vengeance, and he kept his vow. In the first days of spring a large army was despatched against the rebel Poles under General Chlopicki, who, while in command of the thirteenth and fourteenth Army Corps, had earned for his troops the nickname of the Lions of Varna. The war was waged to the death. The Russian troops, well drilled and ably commanded, elated with the successes of the past, met the untutored Polish soldiers with a confidence bred of conceit.

The Poles, imbued with a sense of patriotism, and recognising that it was to do or to die, fought each man for his own hand, neither giving nor expecting quarter, and the slaughter was frightful. Even at Ostralenka, where the Poles left seven thousand dead on the field, the Russian loss was over fifteen thousand; and at Waror the Poles took ten thousand Russian prisoners, besides a number of cannon, which were exhibited in the streets of Warsaw, amid the enthusiastic applause of the inhabitants.

After being beaten all along the line the Russian Army withdrew, leaving the flower of its surviving officers imprisoned in Warsaw, and for a while the Poles had rest. But only for a while. In the early summer, another army marched on the capital, and at the end of June General Paskewitsch, who had been specially chosen by the *Czar*, took the command. This officer enjoyed the personal friendship of the ruler of Russia, and he took the field with the express instruction from his master to teach the rebels a lesson which they would not forget. He lost no time in resuming operations, but changed his predecessor's plans. Hitherto, all attempts on Warsaw had been made from the right bank of the Vistula. With the exception of the Praga suburb the city lies on the left or south bank, so that to capture it from the north the Russians would have to fight their way across the Vistula either through the streets and across the bridges of Praga, or under the fire of the guns in the Polish works.

Paskewitsch decided upon making a flank march down the right bank of the river, crossing it near the Prussian frontier, where he had secretly arranged to obtain supplies and bridging material from the Prussian fortress of Thorn, and then marching up the south bank of the Vistula he could attack Warsaw on the side on which it was not protected by the broad river which had hitherto barred the Russian

OLD TOWN, WARSAW

THE JEWS' MARKET, WARSAW.

advance. The Polish Government was at this period presided over by General Skryznecki, a patriot of good family and education, and a man of the highest principle. Skryznecki recognised the danger too late. He hurriedly occupied a strong position on the line of the Bzura River with 30,000 men, in the hope of barring the Russian advance; but on August 15th the Russians, in overwhelming force, drove the Poles from the river bank and forced them back upon Warsaw. Their city was now threatened by 60,000 troops, who cut them off from the country to the south of the Vistula, from which they had hitherto drawn supplies and reinforcements. While Paskewitsch thus hemmed in the Poles on the south, another Russian Army watched Praga; and thus, by the end of August, while the roads for miles round were guarded by Russian legions, the Poles found themselves shut in like rats in a trap.

And now for the first time the Poles realised their position. Surrounded by a relentless horde, their supplies cut off, they realised the futility of the claims of a just cause against the exigencies of necessity. The whole of the resources of Russia were against them; and while the sympathies of France and England went far to cheer the desperate band of patriots who yet fought for freedom, the fact that Prussia, though nominally a neutral state, was aiding the common enemy, was not reassuring. So far back as June this fact had been known, and General Skryznecki had written to the King of Prussia enumerating the various acts indulged in by his ministers, and demanding that they should cease. In this historic document the general proved that the Prussians were supplying the Russians with food from the storehouses at Thorn, that they had lent their skilled artillery to the Russians, that they had supplied ammunition and uniforms made in Prussia, and that most of the engineering works required by the Russians—including the bridge over the Vistula—had been executed by German engineers.

This letter was never answered, and Prussia continued in her breach of the laws of war, while the outlook in Warsaw became blacker every day. Nor were the dangers only from without. The Polish mob began to become turbulent, and necessitated the watching of soldiers who would have been better employed negotiating the enemy. But even these measures were insufficient to keep the rough element down. The irresistible descent of the Russian Army was the excuse for an outcry against the noble Skyznecki; and in the hope of uniting the besieged he resigned his command of the Polish army, General Dembinski being appointed in his place.

But even this step did not succeed in quieting the rabble. On the night of the 15th August the mob rose and marched to the State prison, where Russian officers who had been taken prisoners in the war had been incarcerated. The excitement of the mob was intense. Their blood was up, and this is the only excuse that can be urged for the foulest deed that blemishes the history of Poland. The gates of the prison were forced, and the prisoners led out and shamefully ill-treated. The crowd behaved like wild beasts, chasing and attacking the unfortunate Russians; and after being tortured in every way that occurred to the imagination of their captors, the miserable beings were butchered in the streets, the gutters literally running in blood. Among the victims of this tragedy were four Russian generals and several ladies of high birth, who had been suspected of sympathising with the enemy. All were brutally murdered, the atrocities being continued for two days. At length order was restored by the military, who were withdrawn from the defence of the city for this purpose.

While these events were taking place within the city General Paskewitsch was pressing on in pursuit of the Polish Army, which he had compelled to retreat from the Bzura. But even here the defenders were unable to hold their ground, and on the 1st of September they retired behind the entrenchments which had been thrown up immediately before Warsaw. Here the final stand had to be made. The headquarters of the Russians was only three miles away from the city walls, and the capital was threatened on every side. The position was, in short, so acute that it is a matter of some surprise that the Poles did not retire within the city and stand a siege. This question has been ably discussed by a trustworthy historian, M. Brozozowski, who writes as follows:—

It would have been very easy, for the army to defend itself within the walls and from house to house. It had already performed more difficult feats, and Europe doubtless would have rung with its heroism if, after the example of Saragossa, it had buried itself under the ruins of Warsaw. But the Poles could not, for the sake of a mere empty renown, consent to the destruction of a city which is the hearth-stone of their patriotism and the centre of their nationality—a city which in future struggles is yet destined to play an important part, for the Poles are far from succumbing under their present misfortunes—very far from abandoning the hope of again becoming a nation. (*La*

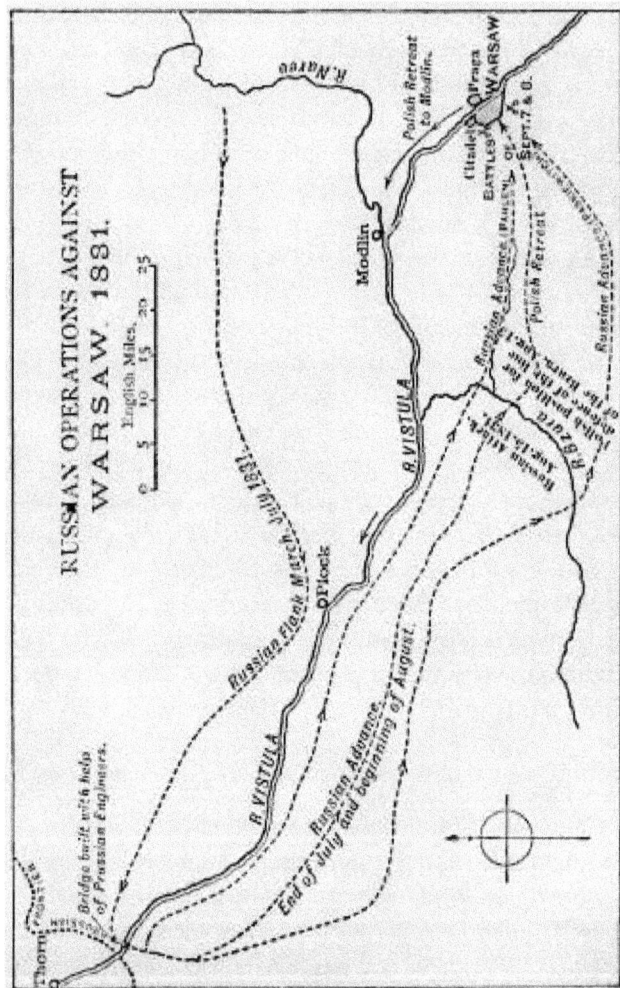

RUSSIAN OPERATIONS AGAINST WARSAW. 1831.

Guerre de la Pologne)

But still, the attacking army waited before striking the final blow. Reinforcements from the south were expected. Several days were wasted pending their arrival, and when they arrived their pontoons stuck in the mud. But Paskewitsch did not mind the delay. He is reported to have said to one of his staff, "I await the aid of two armies—the army of the south and the army of famine." Nor were these expectations vain. While beleaguered from without, the doomed city was ravaged within. Gaunt famine marched unchecked through the fine streets, and starvation claimed more victims than did shot or shell.

Then it was that, recognising all resistance as futile, the Poles attempted to open negotiations with the enemy; but the mob would not have it, and the overtures made were cancelled in order to prevent a revolution, while an offer of terms made by Paskewitsch was rejected for a similar reason.

These preliminaries over, the attack upon Warsaw began in earnest on the morning of the 6th September. The fighting on this day was mostly at long range, but the Russian attack was so strong and the firing so fierce that the Poles had to abandon their first line of entrenchment. The assault then ceased, and both sides rested during the night; but at daybreak on the 7th the attack was renewed, and the slaughter was terrible. The Poles—especially the battalions occupying the redoubt on the Wola side of the Vistula—made an heroic resistance. The

EMPEROR NICHOLAS.

Russians had on this day no fewer than 386 guns in position, and the fire from them was so fierce and so continuous that nothing could stand before it.

The Poles were ploughed down by the hail of projectiles, and those spared by the shells were despatched by small arms. After some hours of bombardment, when a mere handful of the garrison of the Wola redoubt remained, the Russians closed up in their strength and charged with their bayonets. The result was disastrous in the extreme. General Sowinski, who commanded the outpost, fell pierced through and through; and when the Russians finally occupied the redoubt only eleven men remained alive out of three thousand.

While this scene of carnage was being enacted outside, the city was itself the scene of intense excitement. The majority of the inhabitants foresaw that their fate was sealed. Their only chance of salvation—the interposition of England or France—had failed them. Were even that to come now it would be too late. The cannonade of the besiegers was continuous, and every now and again a stray shell would fall in the streets, scattering death and devastation. around. And all that could be done in response was to fire occasional charges from the few guns left to the garrison. Men there were in plenty in Warsaw, and women, too, willing to play the man's part in fighting for their country; but the guns were few, and it was no uncommon sight to see eager, able men tear the rifles from the hands of the wounded as they fell, in order that the most might be made of the slender sources at their disposal.

Amid all this scene of horror there was one item of news which caused rejoicing. Marshal Paskewitsch had been wounded. It was said that he was, indeed, disabled. This was the one cheering event of the 7th September.

The 8th opened still and fine, but it was destined to be a bitter day in the story of Poland.

The Russians had moved up to the very gates of the town in the night, and only the innermost line of trenches and the shaky walls stood between them and the inhabitants. The cannonade re-commenced soon after daybreak, and the attack was even more furious than on the previous day. At least, it seemed so to those within the doomed city. The men in the trenches were ploughed down like flies, but their bravery was indomitable, and as each man fell, another took his place, to be ploughed down in turn. The men finally stood upon the brink of their trenches, and used the dead bodies of their comrades as cover; but it was futile. On and on came the Russian host,

THE RUSSIANS CLOSED UP IN THEIR STRENGTH
AND CHARGED WITH THEIR BAYONETS

back and back went the Poles, until only the gaunt walls of Warsaw stood between them and those they sought to save. The enemy fought with irresistible fury, carrying everything before them, inch by inch, at the point of the bayonet, while their guns were busied in sending missiles within the city, which spread fire and rapine in their train. The day was still undone when the walls were gained. The inmost line of defence was captured, its last defender slain. The plain for a mile around was strewn with the mutilated remains of what had once been brave men, and the tyrants of the North held Warsaw in their hands.

The city capitulated as the sun sunk in the west, and its inhabitants realised too late that their doom was sealed. What that doom was to be even the most imaginative failed to realise.

Having taken Warsaw, Paskewitsch spoke fair. He would, he declared, not enter the city till the following day, and meanwhile the Polish Army, what was left of it, might retire to Plosk. The Marshal admitted to having 3,000 men and 63 officers killed, and 7,500 and 445 officers wounded, while the Polish loss was found to amount to 9,000 slain.

Defeated though they were, reduced in numbers, without the hope of succour, and exhausted by the events of the past few days, the Poles retained their heroism. The army, what was left of the 30,000 men of which the garrison had consisted, formed in order in the great place in the centre of the city, and marched towards the gate. But it did not march to Plosk. It went instead to the fortress of Modlin, and made preparations for a final stand—a forlorn hope—trusting to fortune to turn the Russians yet. But the scheme was foredoomed. Paskewitsch, whose wound was slighter than was supposed, heard of the move, and promptly despatched a brigade against the Polish remnant. The garrison of Modlin was promptly surrounded, all retreat cut off. Entrapped, defenceless, without guns or food, the band of heroes lay down their arms and sought refuge on neutral territory across the Prussian frontier.

It does not come within the province of this history to detail the events which followed the capture of Warsaw. So far as the military history of this, the last great struggle for Polish independence, is concerned, the battle of Warsaw brings the story to a close. The horrors that followed still linger in the memories of the very old. The fearful outbreak of Asiatic cholera which devastated Central Europe, the tragic fate of the thousands of Poles who, trusting in the charity of the King of Prussia, were hounded across the frontier into the hands of the Russians; the equally tragic fortunes of those who took the word of the *Czar* and gave themselves up to the authorities; and the bitter savageries committed by the Russians in compulsorily emigrating the bulk of the people of Warsaw, sending children away from parents and husbands from wives, even to the furthest parts of Eastern Russia, are all part of history. Of the civilising efforts of the Russians while in occupation of Warsaw, we have a sample in the fact that the conquerors took nearly a million volumes of books from the city—400,000 from the Zuluski Library alone.

LEONAUR

ALSO FROM LEONAUR
AVAILABLE IN SOFTCOVER OR HARDCOVER WITH DUST JACKET

THE WOMAN IN BATTLE *by Loreta Janeta Velazquez*—Soldier, Spy and Secret Service Agent for the Confederacy During the American Civil War.

BOOTS AND SADDLES *by Elizabeth B. Custer*—The experiences of General Custer's Wife on the Western Plains.

FANNIE BEERS' CIVIL WAR *by Fannie A. Beers*—A Confederate Lady's Experiences of Nursing During the Campaigns & Battles of the American Civil War.

LADY SALE'S AFGHANISTAN *by Florentia Sale*—An Indomitable Victorian Lady's Account of the Retreat from Kabul During the First Afghan War.

THE TWO WARS OF MRS DUBERLY *by Frances Isabella Duberly*—An Intrepid Victorian Lady's Experience of the Crimea and Indian Mutiny.

THE REBELLIOUS DUCHESS *by Paul F. S. Dermoncourt*—The Adventures of the Duchess of Berri and Her Attempt to Overthrow French Monarchy.

LADIES OF WATERLOO *by Charlotte A. Eaton, Magdalene de Lancey & Juana Smith*—The Experiences of Three Women During the Campaign of 1815: Waterloo Days by Charlotte A. Eaton, A Week at Waterloo by Magdalene de Lancey & Juana's Story by Juana Smith.

NURSE AND SPY IN THE UNION ARMY *by Sarah Emma Evelyn Edmonds*—During the American Civil War

WIFE NO. 19 *by Ann Eliza Young*—The Life & Ordeals of a Mormon Woman During the 19th Century

DIARY OF A NURSE IN SOUTH AFRICA *by Alice Bron*—With the Dutch-Belgian Red Cross During the Boer War

MARIE ANTOINETTE AND THE DOWNFALL OF ROYALTY *by Imbert de Saint-Amand*—The Queen of France and the French Revolution

THE MEMSAHIB & THE MUTINY *by R. M. Coopland*—An English lady's ordeals in Gwalior and Agra duringthe Indian Mutiny 1857

MY CAPTIVITY AMONG THE SIOUX INDIANS *by Fanny Kelly*—The ordeal of a pioneer woman crossing the Western Plains in 1864

WITH MAXIMILIAN IN MEXICO *by Sara Yorke Stevenson*—A Lady's experience of the French Adventure

www.ingramcontent.com/pod-product-compliance
Lightning Source LLC
Chambersburg PA
CBHW030013110426
42741CB00032B/496